WALKING IN CARMARTHENSHIRE

About the Author

Jim Rubery now resides in South West Wales, where he and his wife run a small caravan park in the Pembrokeshire National Park. He has always been a very keen participant in outdoor pursuits, spending a great deal of his time over the years rock climbing, mountaineering, skiing, walking and canoeing, and has also dabbled with caving and sailing.

His writing career, mainly centered on climbing articles and climbing guides, started in the early 1990s when living in Yorkshire. However, he soon expanded into the walking world with a regular feature in *Yorkshire Life*, *Lancashire Life*, *Cheshire Life* and *Lake District Life* magazines, entitled 'Rambling with Rubery'. In 2004 Jim moved to Hertfordshire where he continued the walking trend with articles for *Hertfordshire Life* and *Essex Life* magazines. Over the years he has had a number of walking books published, covering Cheshire, the Yorkshire Dales, the Lake District and the Peak District.

Other Cicerone guides by the author

Historic Walks in Cheshire
Historic Walks in North Yorkshire

WALKING IN CARMARTHENSHIRE

by Jim Rubery

2 POLICE SQUARE, MILNTHORPE, CUMBRIA LA7 7PY
www.cicerone.co.uk

© Jim Rubery 2015
First edition 2015
ISBN: 978 1 85284 737 1

Printed by KHL Printing, Singapore

A catalogue record for this book is available from the British Library.
All photographs are by the author unless otherwise stated.

Updates to this Guide

While every effort is made by our authors to ensure the accuracy of guidebooks as they go to print, changes can occur during the lifetime of an edition. Any updates that we know of for this guide will be on the Cicerone website (www.cicerone.co.uk/737/updates), so please check before planning your trip. We also advise that you check information about such things as transport, accommodation and shops locally. Even rights of way can be altered over time. We are always grateful for information about any discrepancies between a guidebook and the facts on the ground, sent by email to info@cicerone.co.uk or by post to Cicerone, 2 Police Square, Milnthorpe LA7 7PY, United Kingdom.

Front cover: Carreg Cennan Castle

CONTENTS

Route symbols on OS map extracts
(for OS legend see printed OS maps)

- route
- shortcut/diversion
- extension
- start/finish point
- start point
- finish point
- route direction

Features on the overview map

- County/Unitary boundary
- Urban area
- National Park

800m
600m
400m
200m
75m
0m

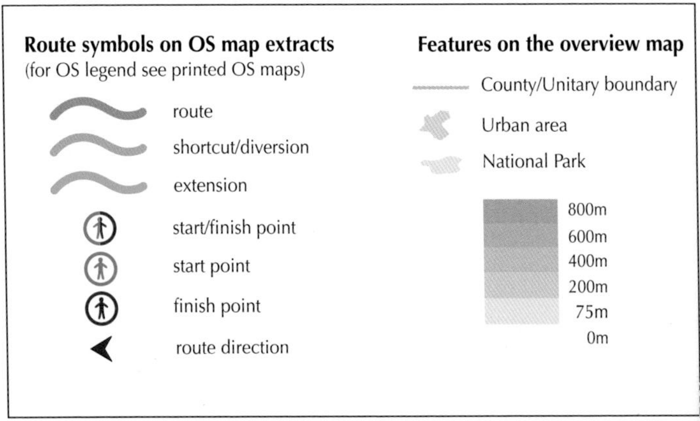

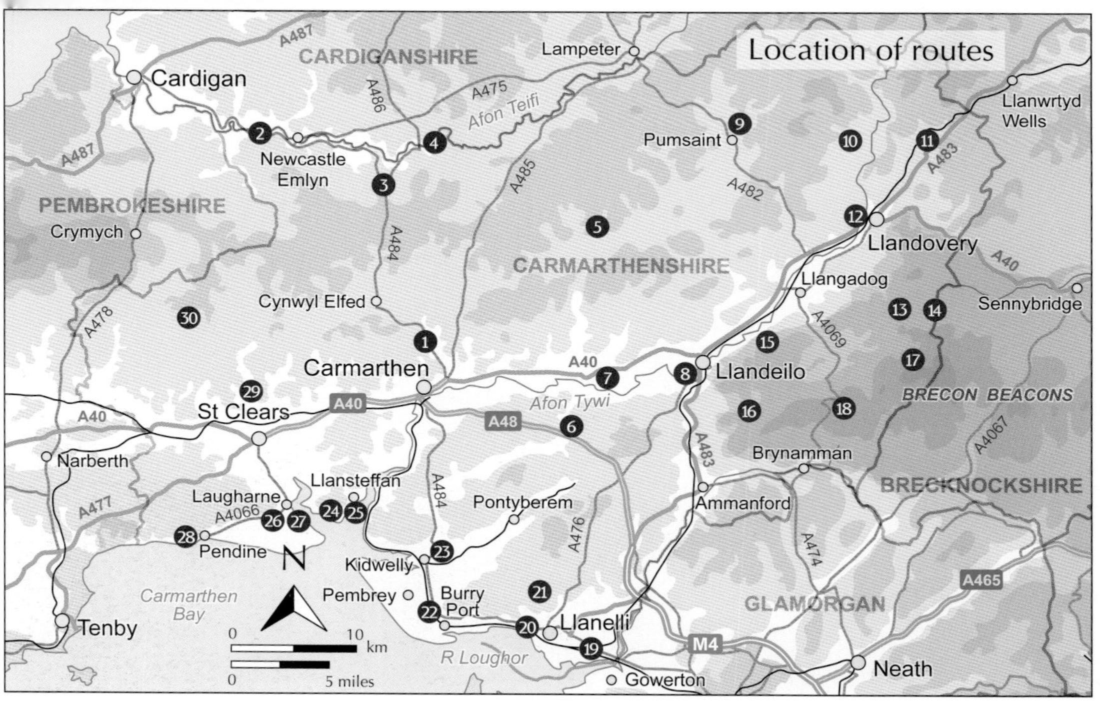
Location of routes
Cardigan
Newcastle Emlyn
Lampeter
Pumsaint
Llanwrtyd Wells
Llandovery
Llangadog
Sennybridge
Crymych
Cynwyl Elfed
Carmarthen
Llandeilo
St Clears
Narberth
Llansteffan
Laugharne
Pendine
Kidwelly
Pembrey
Burry Port
Pontyberem
Ammanford
Brynamman
Llanelli
Gowerton
Neath
Tenby
CARDIGANSHIRE
PEMBROKESHIRE
CARMARTHENSHIRE
BRECON BEACONS
BRECKNOCKSHIRE
GLAMORGAN
Afon Teifi
Afon Tywi
R Loughor
Carmarthen Bay
A487
A486
A475
A485
A482
A483
A40
A484
A478
A48
A4069
A4067
A477
A4066
A476
A474
A465
M4
N
0
10
km
0
5 miles
1
2
3
4
5
6
7
8
9
10
11
12
13
14
15
16
17
18
19
20
21
22
23
24
25
26
27
28
29
30

Stile in the upper reaches of the Tywi Valley

INTRODUCTION

The very pleasant footpath through Coed y Castle (Walk 16)

With vast stretches of golden sands, breathtaking mountain scenery, fast-flowing rivers, quiet upland lakes, pretty market towns, isolated farmsteads, extensive tracts of forest, evocative castle ruins, empty country lanes and a rich industrial heritage, it is not surprising that Carmarthenshire is one of the most beautiful counties in Britain. Add to this the fact that it has around 3000km of footpaths, bridleways, green lanes and byways, the vast majority of which are well kept, clearly waymarked and furnished to a high standard with gates and stiles, it is hardly surprising that it is a paradise for walkers who can explore these gems at their leisure.

Carmarthenshire is often overlooked by visitors, as they speed ever westward along the M4 and A40 towards its southwesterly neighbour, Pembrokeshire. To many, it's not so much a place to terminate the journey and explore but more that bit to pass through between Swansea and St Clears. In some ways this is a real shame because the county is stunningly beautiful with a rich diversity of landscapes. For the discerning walker, however, who has already discovered the treasures of Carmarthenshire, it is something to celebrate, as the footpaths, tracks and bridleways remain largely peaceful and devoid of people.

Covering some 2398 sq km (11.5 percent of total Wales land mass), Carmarthenshire, or to give it its correct Welsh name, Sir Gaerfyrddin, is the third largest county in Wales. It has always been a large county, and up to 1974 held the accolade as the largest in Wales. During that year, following a seriously provocative set of boundary and authority changes, Carmarthenshire ceased to exist, being swallowed up, along with Pembrokeshire and Cardiganshire, in the new county of Dyfed. In 1996 it reappeared, following a further bout of reorganisation and boundary change; not quite in its original guise, but the one that we see today.

It is a county of great contrasts, stretching from the sandy beaches of Carmarthen Bay in the south to the empty uplands of the Cambrian Mountains in the north; from the high mountains of Y Mynydd Du in the east to the gently rolling farmland, along the Pembrokeshire border, in the west. Agricultural landscapes predominate, but among the folds of the hills and along the river valleys, there is a good spattering of pretty market towns, all of which are friendly, full of character and offer a range of places for refreshment or accommodation. The most extensive urban landscape occupies the southeastern corner of the county, an area that is also home to 65 percent of its resident population, who live in or around the towns of Llanelli and Burry Port, now both transformed from their industrial past.

LANDSCAPE AND GEOLOGY

As with the rest of Britain, the geological events that initially shaped Carmarthenshire occurred hundreds of millions of years ago, south of the equator and beneath warm tropical seas. For the past 425 million years, the continental plate, on which we stand, has been drifting imperceptibly northwards. For the most part, the exposed rocks of Carmarthenshire are sedimentary and consist largely of a mixture of shales, conglomerates, sandstones and mudstones, with Millstone Grit and Carboniferous Limestone forming the northwestern rim of the South Wales coalfield, which extends into Carmarthenshire in the southeast of the county, but which is also exposed in the sea cliffs running westward from Pendine towards Pembrokeshire.

Almost the whole of the county is hilly or mountainous, the exception being the southern coastal fringes. On its eastern borders, abutting the county of Neath-Port Talbot and Swansea, rise the imposing range of the Mynydd Du (the Black Mountains) and the westernmost part of the Brecon Beacons, where the county's 'top' can be found in the shapely form of Fan Foel, standing at a proud 781m (2562ft). These north facing escarpments are formed from Old Red Sandstone, rocks of

Creek and mudflats near Burry Port (Walk 22)

Palaeozoic age that were moulded, like the rest of Wales, during the late Tertiary period when they were thrust skyward to form hills and mountains. Glacial erosion during the Pleistocene ice ages greatly modified their contours, along with wind, rain and snow in more recent times. Outcrops of Millstone Grit and Carboniferous Limestone add to the geological mix. The area also forms part of the Fforest Fawr Geopark, the first of its kind in Wales, set up to promote the wealth of natural and cultural interest in the area. Here, as elsewhere in Wales, there is a high degree of correlation between rocks and relief.

In the north of the county, adjoining Ceredigion and Powys, rise the Cambrian Mountains of Mid Wales, one of the largest expanses of wilderness south of Scotland and largely composed of sedimentary sandstones and mudstones. Their geological history is not dissimilar to the Myndd Du, but their current features are the product of thousands of years of interaction between an exposed upland environment and the few communities that have succeeded in creating their livelihood there. In the past, the name 'Cambrian Mountains' was applied in a general sense to most of upland Wales, including Snowdonia and the Brecon Beacons. During the 1950s, the name became synonymous with the homogenous upland region of Mid Wales that includes Pumlumon in the north of the region, Elenydd in the middle and Mynydd Mallaen in the south. Due to its beauty and unspoilt nature, in 1965 the National Parks Commission proposed the area be given National Park status, although this has not happened.

It is the southern part of the Cambrian Mountains that lies within Carmarthenshire's borders, a vast expanse of rolling hills and quiet valleys comprising the Mynydd Llanllwni, Mynydd Mallaen and Rhandirmwyn, where the bleat of sheep, the splashing of streams and the call of the red kite and buzzard are likely to be all you hear as you roam these empty landscapes. Two of Carmarthenshire's principal rivers rise in these mountains, the Teifi, a spectacular river and one of the most important rivers for wildlife, which forms the northern county boundary with Ceredigion. The other is the Tywi, a remarkably beautiful river that flows for 121km before emptying into the brackish waters of Carmarthen Bay at Llansteffan, navigable since Roman times.

The west of the county is more rolling and largely given over to beef and dairy farming. It is also where you will find the county town, Carmarthen, the most important town in west Wales for almost 2000 years and the oldest continuously occupied settlement in the whole of Wales since Roman times.

The south of the county is bordered by Carmarthen Bay, abutted to the east by the Gower Area of Outstanding National Beauty and

The long track beneath the northern slopes of Y Mynydd Du (Walk 18)

to the east by Pembrokeshire Coast National Park. In between these two 'book ends' lie 129km of golden sandy beaches, ever changing river estuaries, awe-inspiring castles and pretty coastal towns, now all linked by the Carmarthenshire section of the Wales Coast Path. It is here that the largest town in the county can be found, Llanelli, situated in its south-eastern corner, on the Loughor Estuary and famous for its proud rugby tradition, but also for its tinplate industry. It is in this area that Carmarthenshire's chief coal deposits were found, an extension of the South Wales coalfield, with most of the mining occurring in the Gwendraeth Valley and Llanelly districts. The county has few other mineral deposits of note. Limestone was quarried and burnt in the Black Mountains, mainly for agricultural use, but metallic ores are rare, with small quantities of iron-ore being mined in the hills around Llandeilo and Llandovery and much smaller quantities of gold being extracted near Pumsaint.

HISTORY

Carmarthenshire is dotted with prehistoric remains, including burial chambers, standing stones, hill forts, tumuli and stone circles, very few of which have been excavated adequately and few of these have been dated scientifically. One exception is Coygan Cave, a limestone cave near Laugharne, now destroyed by quarrying but which was extensively excavated and produced archaeological finds that included two hand axes of Mousterian type associated with Neanderthals, from about 50,000 years ago. Other palaeo-ecological work has shown that human exploitation of this region occurred from round about this time, albeit with varying and uneven intensity, but particularly the expansion of activity from the late Neolithic, which can be equated with a general growth in settlement and agriculture, similar to the rest of the British Isles.

When the Romans invaded Britannia in AD43, Carmarthenshire formed part of the lands of the Demetae tribe, a Celtic people of the late Iron Age. Following their submission, the Romans built a fort at Carmarthen, Moridunum, followed by others at Loughor, Llandeilo and Llandovery. They also had a settlement at the Dolaucothi Gold Mines near Pumsaint.

When the Romans departed, South Wales returned to the same structure of small, independent kingdoms as in the Iron Age, with the Demetae taking control of Carmarthenshire, enlarging the town of Moridunum and using it as their capital, thus making it the oldest, continually inhabited settlement in Wales. The town eventually became known as Caerfyrddin, anglicized into Carmarthen, which subsequently gave its name to the county.

During the fifth and sixth centuries, Carmarthenshire's inhabitants became more civilised and were also introduced to doctrines of Christianity, thanks to a group of hard working Celtic missionaries, notably St David and St Teilo. In the ninth and 10th centuries, the influx of Irish from the west and British from the east began to test the tribal boundaries and in AD920, Hywel Dda, the prince of South Wales, scrapped old kingdoms and created four new ones, Gwent, Gwynedd, Powys and Deheubarth, the latter including the region of Carmarthenshire.

In 1080 the Normans first appeared on the shores of Carmarthen Bay and following numerous skirmishes, conquered Deheubarth in 1093. By the end of King Henry I's reign, in 1135, the great castles of Kidwelly, Carmarthen, Laugharne and Llanstephan had been constructed. Although the former kingdom of Deheubarth briefly re-emerged in the 12th century under Maredudd ap Gruffydd and the Lord Rhys, the Normans soon re-exerted control and Deheubarth ceased to exist as a kingdom after 1234. By the Statutes of Rhuddlan (1284), Edward I formed the counties of Cardigan and Carmarthen and in the ensuing years, the prosperity of the new county increased considerably, resulting in Edward III naming Carmarthen as the foremost town in Wales for the wool trade.

In the reign of Henry IV, Owain Glyndwr, the last of the Welsh Princes, upset the apple cart for a time, having obtained the assistance of an army of

Afon Teifi at Cenarth (Walk 2)

Old barns at Ty hen (Walk 3)

12,000 men from France and, being joined by several of the Welsh chieftains, he set about regaining control of the country. Unfortunately for him, his battle plan was flawed, particularly with regard to a lack of artillery to defend his strongholds and ships to protect the coastline, and in 1409 he was driven out of the area by the superior resources of the English. Amazingly, he was never captured, despite a huge ransom on his head.

Following the Civil War in the 17th century, the castles of Carmarthenshire that had supported the royal cause soon fell to the parliamentarian forces, resulting in Cromwell ordering their dismantling and so preventing their use in any further skirmishes.

In the ensuing years, the great Welsh spiritual and educational movement had its roots in the little village of Llanddowror, where the celebrated and pious vicar, Griffith Jones, had become the founder of the Welsh circulating charity schools.

NATURE RESERVES AND WILDLIFE HABITATS

In a county as large as Carmarthenshire, and with so many diverse habitats, it is not surprising that nature and wildlife is well catered for. The county is justly renowned for its magnificent coast, quiet estuaries, steep wooded valleys and vast expanses of mountain and moorland. On top of this there are hundreds of kilometres of hedgerow and hedgebank, many of which are of historical importance. With the patchwork of woodlands throughout the county and the thousands of acres of fields, it soon becomes evident that the biodiversity is huge. Add to this the rich abundance of species that live in the sea and on the seabed around the Carmarthenshire coast and the wildlife habitats increase even more.

The Mynydd Du, in the east of the county, falls largely within the boundaries of the Brecon Beacons National Park and all the protection legislation that that affords. There are 12 nature reserves, cared for by the Wildlife Trust of South and West Wales and 81 Sites of Special Scientific Interest (SSSI), covering over 17,000ha and ranging in size from small fields to long rivers, disused quarries to large areas of mountainside, and this excludes the ones that are found in the Carmarthenshire part of Brecon Beacons National Park. There are two Special Protection Areas (SPA) and seven Special Areas of Conservation (SAC), sites considered to be of international importance for nature conservation. Carmarthenshire also has five Local Nature Reserves (LNRs), sites designated by local authorities as supporting a rich variety of wildlife or geological features and which allow local people contact with the natural environment. The RSPB have a reserve at Gwenffrwd-Dinas, in the north of the county and there is also the splendid National Wetlands Centre Wales,

The magnificent ruins of Laugharne Castle (Walk 26)

Market hall, Laugharne (Walk 26)

on the Bury Inlet, where it is possible to see wild birds up to 50,000 strong during the winter months.

TRANSPORT

Swansea, Llanelli and Carmarthen are the main transport hubs in the area, all being on the inter-city route from London Paddington to South and West Wales. The Heart of Wales Railway Line, although not as fast or as frequent, links Shrewsbury to Swansea, calling at Llandovery, Llandeilo, Ammanford and several other stops before terminating in Swansea.

The M4 motorway and the A48 dual carriageway run east to west through the county, while the A40 runs northeast to southwest, passing along the Tywi Valley and through Carmarthen and St Clears. There is also an extensive network of other A-roads and numerous minor roads throughout the county, with good access to all the major towns and villages. There is an excellent bus service, particularly between the main towns, and even many of the remote villages have a service, although these may not be as frequent and non-existent on a Sunday.

See Appendix B for useful contact telephone numbers and website links.

STAYING IN CARMARTHENSHIRE

Carmarthenshire is a recognised tourist destination and as such is well served with all types of accommodation, including B&Bs, hotels, self catering options and many caravan, camping and even glamping sites. The seaside resorts are very popular and tend to book up early for the main school holiday weeks. Away from the main towns, accommodation is less frequent, particularly in the mountainous areas, where a little forward planning is advised.

For Walks 1–4, 'In and around the Teifi Valley', Newcastle Emlyn would be a suitable base to stay as it has a good range of accommodation, along with Llandysul. For Walks 5–8, 'Castles, gardens and forests', either Carmarthen or Llandeilo would be suitable centres. Llandovery has the most diverse range of accommodation for Walks 9–12 'The Cambrians of Carmarthenshire', and it would also serve as a good base for the Walks 13–18, 'The high mountains of Y Mynydd Du', along with Llandeilo and the towns and villages in the Amman Valley to the south. The area containing Walks 19–23, 'History and heritage', provides the largest choice of places to stay, with Llanelli, Burry Port, Pembrey, Kidwelly and Ferryside all having a range of accommodation providers. Finally, Walks 24–30, 'Dylan Thomas Country' are also well served with Llansteffan, Laugharne, Pendine and St Clears being good bases.

Please refer to Appendix B for details of websites, addresses and telephone numbers that may assist with a stay in Carmarthenshire.

Looking north along Cwm Lliedi Reservoir (Walk 21)

Clockwise from left: common orchids; a wildflower-strewn meadow; cinnabar moth on thistle; rowan berries

WHAT TO TAKE

Much of Carmarthenshire's weather comes winging in on southwesterly air streams, meaning rain is always a possibility, so a good set of quality waterproofs is a must, along with a few spare warm layers for cold or windy days. Also, a number of the walks venture out into high moorland and mountain terrain, where conditions underfoot can get pretty wet, so a stout pair of waterproof boots is also recommended. Because weather conditions can change quite rapidly, particularly on high ground, the appropriate map, a compass and a whistle should also be packed. That said, warm, sunny days are equally likely and the southwesterly air streams tend to bring mild conditions. Because of the county's outstanding array of scenery and prolific wildlife, a camera and binoculars are also worth packing.

'Carmarthenshire Footpaths' sign

MAPS AND WAYMARKING

The walks in this book are covered by seven 1:25,000 Ordinance Survey maps:

- Outdoor Leisure 12 (Brecon Beacons National Park. Western area)
- Explorer 164 (Gower)
- Explorer 177 (Carmarthen & Kidwelly)
- Explorer 178 (Llanelli & Ammanford)
- Explorer 185 (Newcastle Emlyn)
- Explorer 186 (Llandeilo & Brechfa Forest)
- Explorer 187 (Llandovery)

Waymarking is generally very good to excellent, apart from on some of the exposed ridges, moors and mountains, where a map and compass may be necessary; GPS signals are fine in most areas. The furniture on most of the walks is good, with sound stiles and many new pedestrian and kissing gates. Many of the walks pass through woodland where fallen trees may present an obstacle. Where such obstacles were found, mention is made in the text and, if necessary, an alternative route given.

Cenarth (Walk 2)

The Tywi Valley from Carreglwyd (Walk 15)

USING THIS GUIDE

There are 30 walks in this guide, 26 of them being circular and four of them being linear along sections of the Carmarthenshire Coast Path (CCP). The walks are organised into six loosely defined geographical areas. Walks 1–4 cover the north-western area, Walks 5–8 the central region, Walks 9–12 the Cambrian Mountains and upper Tywi Valley, Walks 13–18 the Y Mynydd Du (the Black Mountains), Walks 19–23 the southeastern part along Carmarthen Bay and Walks 24–30 the southwestern corner and holiday resorts along that stretch of coast.

Some are relatively short excursions that can easily be completed in a few hours, while others require considerably more time and can be quite challenging as they head out into open country, where knowledge of map and compass use is highly recommended.

The time needed to complete the walks will vary, depending on fitness, experience and even the composition of a party, should there be several people attempting a walk together. However, it is roughly based on a person being of reasonable fitness and able to cover around 2mph.

In places, it's possible to link some of the walks together to make a lengthier outing, or even to shorten some, should time be an issue. Where this is the case, there is mention of the fact in the introductory paragraph to the walks concerned. The four linear walks, along the CCP, all have good bus or rail (or both) links back to the start.

Routes are illustrated with extracts from the OS 1:50,000 Landranger maps, but it is highly recommended that the relevant 1:25,000 Explorer maps also be referenced and carried. The main route is highlighted in orange, with any alternative route marked in blue. In such cases, the alternative route is described in the main route description. Features along the way that appear on the map are highlighted in bold in the main description.

The contents of this book hardly scratch the surface of the plethora of potential walks that are available in Carmarthenshire, but I hope you enjoy any that you attempt and that it whets your appetite for walking in this fabulous county.

IN AND AROUND THE TEIFI VALLEY

The pretty Nant Tinc on the return leg towards Bronwydd (Walk 1)

WALK 1

Bronwydd and the Gwili Valley

Start/Finish	Bronwydd Village Hall car park (SN 419 246)
Distance	11km (7 miles)
Ascent	260m (855ft)
Time	3–4hrs
Maps	Explorer 177 and 185
Refreshments	Café at Gwili Steam Railway
Public transport	Bus 460 between Carmarthen and Cardigan stops at the Bronwydd Arms. Regular services Mon–Sat, none Sun.

This is a very pleasant walk through an area that was once a hive of industrial activity, with woollen mills, iron forges and corn mills scattered along the banks of the river. The contrast between the valley, where river, road and rail all vie for space in its narrow confines and the quiet expanses of the rolling hill country to the west, is very noticeable. The route initially follows a lovely section of the River Gwili, then crosses the track of the Gwili Steam Railway before climbing steadily along grassy lanes and farm tracks to reach the hamlet of Newchurch. The return is along peaceful lanes, tracks and valley footpaths with a chance to visit the lovingly restored Gwili Steam Railway.

From the car park, pass to the right of the village hall towards the **River Gwili** and go left along a riverside footpath, passing to the right of the cricket ground. This lovely section of footpath above sparkling rapids and stony beaches soon ends at a well placed bench above the river, where it is necessary to turn left over the track bed of the **Gwili Steam Railway** and along the left edge of two fields. At a gate continue ahead, passing to the left of a house to reach the A484 and cross to the far side.

Turn right along the footpath for 150 metres, then go left along a narrow no through road that passes to the right of the chapel. The road climbs steadily up the side of the Nant Cwmdwyfran Valley before swinging right around a sharp U-bend towards farm buildings.

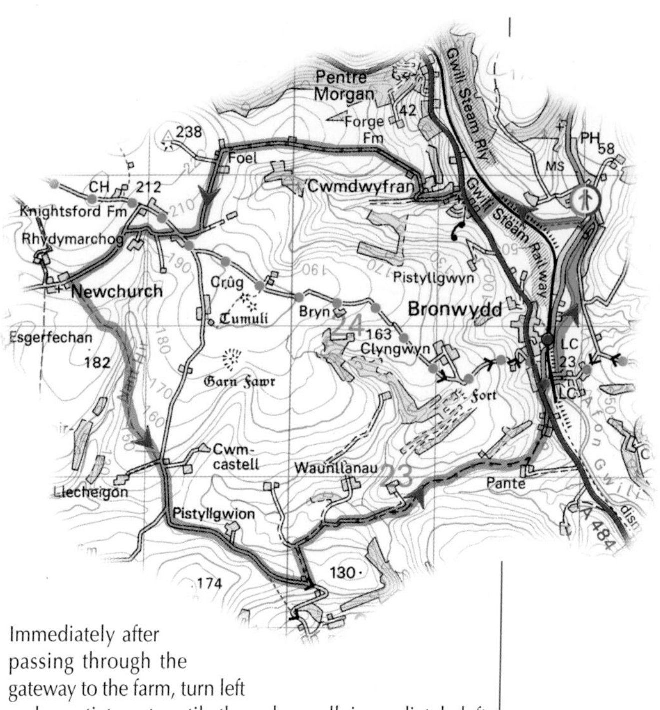

Immediately after passing through the gateway to the farm, turn left and negotiate a step stile through a wall, immediately left of a gate, and follow the stony track ahead as it climbs between fields, revealing some excellent vistas over the Gwili Valley and towards the Black Mountains.

Although the fields surrounding the **Gwili Valley** are well drained and very lush, providing excellent grazing for sheep and cattle, the valley itself was regarded as being too steep sided for normal agricultural use, so much of it has been planted with woodland, large tracts of which can still be seen.

Continue along the track to its end in front of **Foel-fâch Farm** and turn left along a quiet lane, eventually swinging right to reach a T-junction. Go right then almost

St Michael's, Newchurch

immediately left along another lane, passing to the right of the building Ffoslun Uchaf. Follow this short section of lane to another T-junction and here turn left to eventually reach the hamlet of **Newchurch**.

As early as the 12th century, **Newchurch** was known as Eglwys Newydd, suggesting that St Michael's Church, which stands here now, is of Norman origin, but replacing an earlier Celtic church. Two inscribed Christian stones dating from the fifth or sixth century, probably from the earlier church, have been found near here.

Parts of the route here can become a little churned up after wet weather due to lack of drainage and cattle using the bridleway.

On entering the village, turn left immediately before the first house on the left, and follow a pleasant grassy bridleway between high field banks and passing through several gates as it descends into the pretty Nant Hir Valley. Cross the stream and continue ahead, beginning the steady ascent out of the valley. ◂

At the end of the bridleway, turn left along the access drive to **Llecheigon Farm** to reach the road then go right along this for just over 1.5km, with views to the right over Carmarthen in the latter stages. Turn left at a bridleway sign on the left, crossing a cattle grid and joining a concrete access drive that soon descends into the Nant Tinc Valley.

At a fork in the drive, bear right, crossing a cattle grid and following the drive towards Clynmelyn Farm. In the bottom of the valley the drive crosses the Nant Tinc stream and 30 metres beyond this, bear right off the drive, passing through a pair of galvanised gates into a meadow. Go left through the meadow, keeping parallel to the stream, to a stile on the far side and once over bear slightly left along a grassy track between trees, climbing steadily up the side of the valley initially, before descending towards Pante Farm, with fabulous views to the west towards the Brecon Beacons.

Where the track swings sharp right towards **Pante Farm**, turn left and climb a stile beside a gate (waymarker) and walk along the right edge of a sloping field to a stile on the far side, leading onto an access drive to cottages and follow this down to the A484. Cross the A484 to a footpath on the far side and bear left, turning right at the first opportunity at the junction leading to the Gwili Steam Railway. ▶

To visit the railway continue down the road for 350 metres to reach Bronwydd Station on the left where there are toilets and a café.

The **Gwili Railway** is a lovingly restored monument to the nostalgic days of steam that now puffs its way along part of what was formerly the Carmarthen to Aberystwyth railway, which operated for over 100 years until closure in 1965. The Gwili Railway was formed in 1975 and by 1978 had purchased and rescued about 13km of track bed and was running its first steam-hauled service on just over a 1.5km section of what is the first standard-gauge railway to be preserved in Wales. Since then the railway has expanded and currently runs to Danycoed Halt, some 5km northwest of its base at Bronwydd Arms. At the time of writing, the company has begun work

Steaming up on the Gwili line

further south, towards Carmarthen, and has re-laid track to a new station called Carmarthen North built at the old Abergwili junction.

Turn right again after 20 metres and follow the narrow lane steeply down to cross the railway line followed by the **River Gwili**. Immediately on the far side of the bridge turn left over a stile and join a riverside footpath that runs along the left edge of fields, through a short section of woodland and round the edge of another field, always with the river to the left, before eventually reaching a lane on the outskirts of **Bronwydd**. Go left along the lane to a T-junction and go left over Pont Newydd Bridge, which marks the end of the walk.

WALK 2

Cenarth and Newcastle Emlyn

Start/Finish	Car park, Cenarth Falls (SN 269 416)
Distance	11km (7 miles)
Ascent	305m (1005ft)
Time	3–4hrs
Maps	Explorer 198
Refreshments	Pubs and cafés in Cenarth and Newcastle Emlyn
Public transport	Bus 460 between Carmarthen and Cardigan stops in both Newcastle Emlyn and Cenarth. No services on Sun.

The River Teifi is one of the longest rivers in Wales and recognised as being of international importance for its wildlife. It also forms the county boundary in this part of the country, so the southern half of the walk is in Carmarthenshire, while the northern half steals over the border into Ceredigion. It also visits the spectacular Cenarth Falls and the lovely town of Newcastle Emlyn. It mainly follows clear footpaths, quiet lanes and largely clear tracks, but a problem could lie at the start of the walk when the river is in spate and the riverside footpath is under water; at such times a short section of road can be used to avoid the hazard.

From the car park, join the riverside footpath, passing the spectacular falls and walking along the beautiful wooded gorge of the Afon Teifi. The building on the opposite bank is a 17th-century flour mill, complete with waterwheel. ▶

If the river is in spate and the riverside path inundated, go left along the road for a short distance and take the first turning on the right, opposite the chapel to rejoin the walk in 800 metres.

Cenarth is famous for its **waterfalls**, where salmon can be seen leaping in the autumn as they head up the Teifi to their spawning grounds, and where canoeists pit their skills against the cascades throughout the year. The traditional coracle is still used by fishermen on the river and Cenarth is the home of the National Coracle Centre of Wales.

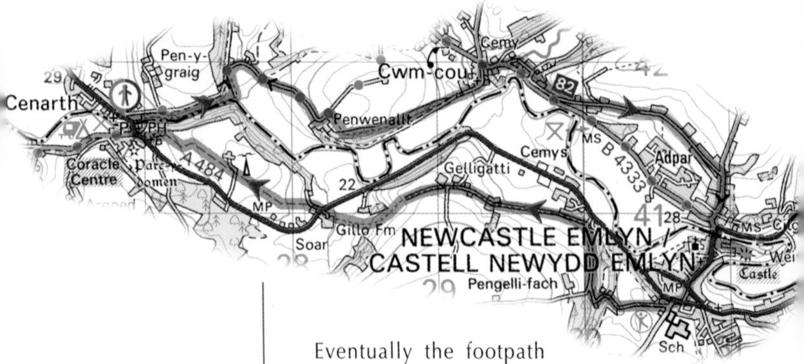

Eventually the footpath swings left, away from the river, climbing gently through the edge of woodland to a junction with a quiet lane (an alternative start joins here), bearing right along it. After negotiating a sharp left bend by **Penwenallt Farm**, continue for a further 150 metres then go right, through a kissing gate in the hedge, cross a field to another kissing gate on the far side and once through, turn left to walk along the top edge of a steeply wooded gorge, with glimpses through the trees of the Teifi Valley to the right. The path eventually begins to descend, emerging onto a farm track, where it is necessary to climb a stone step stile to the left of a gate before proceeding into the hamlet of **Cwm-cou** and a surfaced lane which bends round to the left and a junction with the **B4333**.

Turn sharp right along the road for 200 metres, taking the second lane on the left, signposted as a No Through Road, cross a bridge over the little Afon Ceri and proceed along a surfaced lane through the hamlet of Pont-Ceri, before climbing steadily out of the valley with ever improving views over the Teifi and Newcastle Emlyn to the right. At a T-junction in **Adpar** (site of the first printing press in Wales, set up in 1718) turn right and descend steeply before swinging left to a road junction with the bridge over the river to the right. Join the pedestrian footpath over the bridge and walk up Bridge Street into **Newcastle Emlyn**. ◂

To visit the castle ruins, go left by the old Town Hall in Market Square, continuing along Castle Street to the very artistic entrance to the castle grounds.

Newcastle Emlyn is a busy and bustling town with a market every Friday and an array of small shops, inns, cafés and restaurants. Prior to the building of the castle by Meredith ap Rhys Gryg, on its almost island peninsular in the Teifi Valley in 1240, only a few roughly built cottages stood around the outer banks of the river. Following its construction, a cluster of dwellings sprang up, some for soldiers and Lord Meredith's dependants, others for newcomers and traders to the region seeking both work and protection. All that remains of the castle today is the gate and a few walls, with much of the stone being reclaimed to construct buildings in the town.

Continue along the main street, now Sycamore Street, and go left, passing more shops, pubs and cafés, to just after where the road curves left and here turn right, immediately after passing the Plough Hotel, into Porth Street. At the T-junction at the end, cross the A484, turn right on the opposite side and take the first road on the

Cenarth Bridge over the Afon Teifi

left, signposted to Capel Iwan. After 80 metres, go right along the initially surfaced public bridleway, eventually descending through trees to cross a footbridge beside a ford and, once over, follow the stony track round to the right, climbing energetically through woodland, to reach a lane. Follow the lane to the right, descending to just beyond the Give Way signs, then turn left along a surfaced track to the rear of houses to reach farm buildings. Pass through a waymarked gate to the left of the buildings, continuing along a rough farm track, the first 100 metres of which can be muddy, to reach a stile. Once over, walk down the left side of a field for 300 metres, climb another stile on the left, continuing on the opposite side of the fence, with various fallen boughs and branches that you may have to limbo under or hurdle over before joining the access drive to **Gillo Farm** and a junction with the **A484**.

Cross straight over onto the surfaced public bridleway on the opposite side, but where this curves rightwards towards Gillo-fach, go left along a pleasant track

The attractive entrance to the castle at Newcastle Emlyn

that climbs steadily over the brow of a hill, beneath shady boughs. Pass through two gates in quick succession, that also double as a cattle penning area, continuing along a stony track which is the access drive to Old Vicarage Farm, a very substantial property, and once past this proceed ahead along a grassy track leading to a gate and field. Once through, walk along the left side of the field, descending gently to a pedestrian gate at the bottom and continuing along a sunken footpath between trees, soon passing the Old School House on the right and the church on the left. Bear left on a footpath alongside the wall of the churchyard, descending past The Old Ale House and Three Horseshoes pub to the road. Turn right into **Cenarth**, passing the National Coracle Centre on the right.

The **National Coracle Centre** houses a unique collection of coracles, not only from Wales, but from around the world and gives a fascinating history of the craft. The idea of making a boat by covering a framework of branches with animal hide is a universal one and each region and country adapted their local resources to fit the job. Here in Wales, the earliest coracles used hazel and willow as the framework, preferably covered in horse hide. Later coracles used flannel coated in pitch, tallow or tar, but today's designs use calico with a proofing of pitch. In the early 1860s, the heyday of coracle fishing, there were over 300 boats fishing on the Teifi.

Cross the bridge back to the car park and the start.

WALK 3

Drefach Felindre and the Woollen Trail

Start/Finish	Woollen Mill Museum, Drefach Felindre (SN 355 390)
Distance	10km (6 miles)
Ascent	300m (980ft)
Time	3–4hrs
Maps	Explorer 185
Refreshments	Café at Woollen Mill; pubs in Drefach Felindre
Public transport	Bus 460 between Carmarthen and Cardigan. Frequent services Mon–Sat, none on Sun.

This most interesting walk sets off from the National Wool Museum of Wales in Drefach to follow a series of footpaths and trails through this delightful corner of Carmarthenshire, which became the centre of the Welsh woollen industry during the late 1800s and early 1900s. We visit three rivers, all of which flow into the River Teifi just to the north, but which were key to the development of the woollen industry in this area, both as a source of power to drive the machinery and to scour and wash raw wool and finished fabrics. Although not a particularly long walk, it is fairly arduous, with a number of ascents and descents into and out of the river valleys.

The National Wool Museum is a working museum housed in the former Cambrian Mills and is well worth a visit: it tells the whole story of how sheep have clothed the workers of Wales and the rest of the world.

◂ From the museum, take the footpath that runs parallel to the entrance, crossing a bridge over a stream, but where the track swings rightward towards a house, continue directly ahead through the middle one of three gates and onto a hedge-lined footpath that soon joins a lane. Turn right and follow the lane as it climbs gently for 100 metres, then go sharp left onto a rising footpath through woodland to reach a pedestrian gate in front of a house and here turn left along a track to reach the road on the outskirts of **Waungilwen**.

Cross onto a track on the opposite side of the road and where this forks by Dandinas Farm, keep right, passing low outbuildings and on through quiet woodland with Nant Brân for company to the left. The track passes the ruins of Pant-y-barcud on the left.

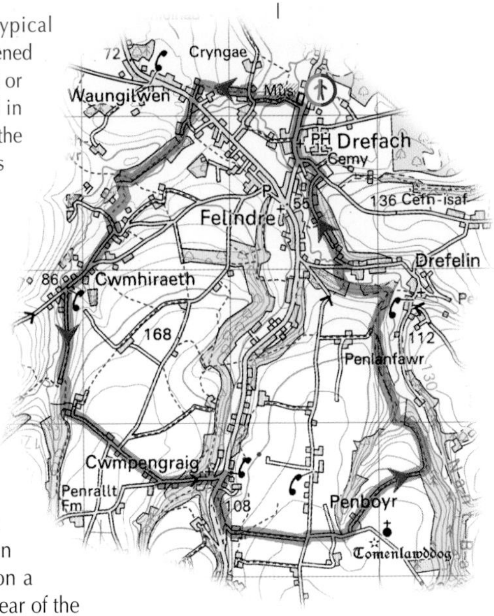

Pant-y-barcud is a typical example of what happened to almost all of the 50 or so mills that operated in this area at the end of the Second World War. As the need for clothes and blankets by the troops dried up, so did the orders from the War Office. The mills closed, the machinery was stripped out and sold for scrap and the buildings began to fall into decay.

Immediately in front of the access gate to an isolated house, go right on a footpath that runs to the rear of the property, keeping left where the path forks to cross three footbridges, eventually joining the access track to a cottage. Go left at the T-junction and follow the track out to a road, which is followed to the right, keeping right at a junction in 350 metres into the hamlet of **Cwmhiraeth**, a former mill village.

Immediately before the bridge over the Nant Brân, bear left along a track, passing a property known as Glanrhyd and immediately in front of the house called Troed-Y-rhiw, bear left onto a footpath running to the rear of the property before climbing steadily through woodland to a junction with a track. Bear right along the track, continuing ahead when it joins a surfaced lane and proceeding directly ahead again after 80 metres, on a continuation track with fine views to the southwest over Moelfre. At a junction with a lane go left and descend quite steeply into the attractive hamlet of **Cwmpengraig**, nestling in the Esgair Valley.

Old mill buildings in Cwmpengraig now make an attractive house

Cwmpengraig was another very important centre for the woollen industry, with several mills in the valley and most of the houses acting as domestic weaving workshops. One of the mills, Coedmor Mill, sited next to the chapel but now a ruin, was the first in the area to develop mechanised carding and spinning mules using water from the Nant Esgair to power the machines. The mill burnt down during the Depression, but was immediately rebuilt, only to burn down again in 1951. Fire was always a major problem in the mills and factories, with all but two of the mills suffering from fires over the years. The problem was that wool is full of lanolin, all the machines relied on heavy grease for lubrication and over time all the timbers in these wooded buildings became impregnated with a mixture of grease and lanolin. Add to this the wool and a highly volatile mixture is created.

Pass **Soar Chapel** on the left, cross the bridge over the Nant Esgair, which is the spawning ground of Sewin (Salmon Trout), walk up to the main road through the valley and bear right along the road to reach the national speed limit signs on the edge of the hamlet. Go left here, off the road, onto a narrow footpath that climbs steeply through woodland to reach a junction with a track and follow this to the left, passing between attractive buildings at Ty hen. Proceed through a gate directly ahead and along a hedge lined track between fields to reach a lane which is followed to the left before taking the first lane on the right which leads to the isolated **Penboyr Church** and the remaining mound of the Norman **Tomen Llawddog Castle.** ▸ Go left through an iron kissing gate just before the farm, joining a grassy track through a pasture just left of farm buildings. Just before reaching the far hedge, bear right to a stile in the corner of the field which gives access to a broad, farm track and go left along this to eventually reach a stile on the left at the termination of the track.

To visit the church and mound, continue past Maesllan Farm for 250 metres.

Once over, join a footpath running through woodland above the Bargod Valley that was known locally as 'The Coffin Trail'.

This footpath passes the site of the **Swigod Arms** (Blue Tit Arms), a hostelry that was a frequent refreshment stop for bearers and mourners as they passed along here on the way to and from funerals at Penboyr Church. Sadly, the pub poured its last drink over 100 years ago!

The path eventually reaches a stile on the left and once over walk round the right edge of a field before descending through more woodland to another stile, giving access to a pasture, which is crossed, to a stile beside a gate on the opposite side. Once over, ford a small stream then swing away rightwards on a grassy track, keeping left where it forks, but where it swings sharp left, back on itself, go right along the top of a steep bank with views to the right over farms and houses on the outskirts of Drefelin. The path soon begins to descend towards the valley, but at a waymarker sign bear left and descend through woodland, going left at the bottom, along a track which zigzags down to the right, then left, before reaching a pedestrian gate leading onto a footpath between fences, soon joining the road through **Drefelin**.

> As the name suggests **Drefelin** (Milltown) was once a bustling village with several mills powered by the Nant Bargod and was known as the Huddersfield of Wales due to its high levels of flannel production; more than any other in Wales. Today, few of the mills remain, but many of the weavers' cottages that lined the road still stand.

Bear right along the road, but immediately after crossing the **Nant Bargod**, go sharp left along a track, going left through an iron kissing gate just beyond the first property on the right and walk along the right edge of two fields with the remnants of an old leet (a manmade mill stream) to the right. Pass through another iron kissing gate and join a lane that runs past the old Dolwion fulling mill, built by the Adams family of Massachusetts. At a T-junction in **Drefach**, alongside the cemetery, turn left down to the main road through the village, then go right along this back to the National Wool Museum.

Drefelin

WALK 4

Llandysul and the Afon Tyweli

Start/Finish	Public car park, Llandysul (SN 418 405)
Distance	11km (7 miles)
Ascent	195m (645ft)
Time	3–4hrs
Maps	Explorer 185
Refreshments	Pubs and cafés in Llandysul
Public transport	Bus 40C Carmarthen–Pencader–Lampeter, then bus 621 Pencader–Llandysul; or bus 460 Carmarthen–Saron–Newcastle Emlyn–Cardigan, then bus 613 Saron–Llandysul (services Wed and Sat only); or bus 612 Newcastle Emlyn–Llandysul (services Tue only).

Starting on the banks of the Afon Teifi, which forms the border between Carmarthenshire and neighbouring Ceredigion (formerly Cardiganshire), the walk quickly crosses the river in the market town of Llandysul, back into the 'home' county. The majority of the walk follows quiet country lanes and a long section of the now dismantled Carmarthen to Cardigan railway that ran along the valley of the pretty Afon Tyweli before joining the Afon Teifi. With only a very short section of potentially boggy ground, this is a suitable walk for the times of year when many footpaths are impassable and traffic along the lanes is at a minimum.

From the public car park in **Llandysul**, walk away from the town on a surfaced footpath, signed to the Picnic Area, with the **church** over to the left and playing fields to the right. The footpath soon runs alongside the Afon Teifi, which forms a looping meander that initially flows away from the town before swinging back towards it. The path eventually bears right, away from the river and passes between houses to join New Road in Llandysul, which is followed to the left and to a junction with Bridge Street.

Llandysul, nestling on the banks of the river Teifi, is a traditional, unspoilt market town that has

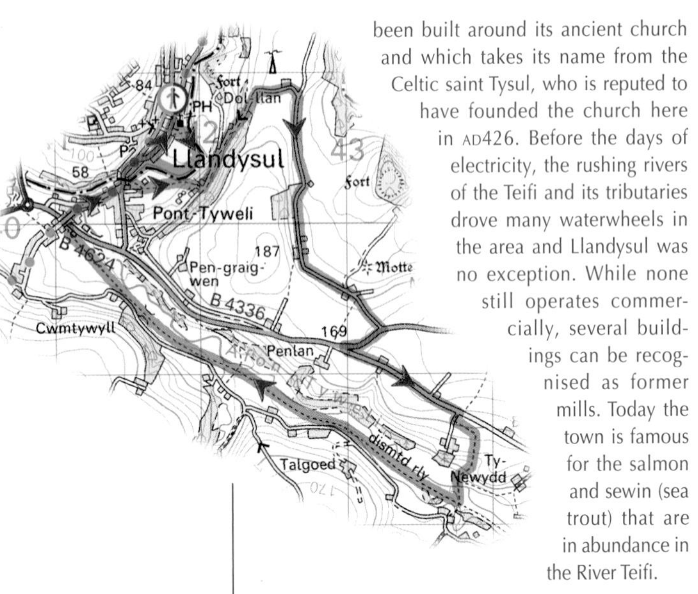

been built around its ancient church and which takes its name from the Celtic saint Tysul, who is reputed to have founded the church here in AD426. Before the days of electricity, the rushing rivers of the Teifi and its tributaries drove many waterwheels in the area and Llandysul was no exception. While none still operates commercially, several buildings can be recognised as former mills. Today the town is famous for the salmon and sewin (sea trout) that are in abundance in the River Teifi.

Go left again, crossing the Afon Teifi via the footpath on the right hand side of the road bridge, which has stood here since the Civil War. The original bridge here was destroyed by Royalists trying to protect the town from being attacked by a force of Cromwell's Roundheads. Set across the river to the right are a series of slalom poles used by the local canoeing centre.

On the far side of the bridge, bear left alongside the first building on the left, currently a canoe hire shop, and walk through its car parking area before bearing slightly right on an initially surfaced footpath that runs to the right of an artificial pond, used by the canoe school for teaching purposes. The path soon becomes un-surfaced and is squeezed in between the river on the left and a fence on the right, before reaching a stile leading into a sloping field. Walk up through this to reach a quiet lane and follow this to the left, passing the entrance to **Dol-llan Farm** before climbing fairly steeply through attractive parkland that forms part of the Dol-llan estate and with improving views along the Teifi Valley. Pass Farmyard on the brow of the hill, once the estate farm to Dol-llan House during the 19th century but now a garden centre, before following the lane round to the right, now with magnificent views to the east along the Teifi Valley.

The site of **Craig Gwrtheyrn**, the Iron Age hill fort, can be seen over to the left. A large tree covered hill, it was originally occupied some 2000 years ago, but later was reputed to be the stronghold of Gwrtheyrn (also known as Vortgern), a powerful king of the Britons during the fifth century.

The lane now begins a gentle descent, passing isolated farms before a junction with the **B4336**. Turn right along this for 300 metres to the next road junction and turn left, following the road to Carmarthen for just over 1km before turning right down the access drive to

Views towards the Cambrian Mountains from near Dol-llan Farm

The lovely Afon Tyweli

Dolmaen Farm. After 75 metres turn left through a gate leading into a field and walk along its top edge, then right down its far edge to pass through a field gate on the left. Once through bear right and go immediately right again through a second gate, then turn left alongside a row of trees to reach a stile over a fence into a steeply sloping pasture punctuated with clumps of bramble and gorse. ▶ Head directly across the next field to the stile and footbridge spanning the **Afon Tyweli** on the far side.

The next section can be boggy, but the best way of avoiding most of the wet area is to traverse across the pasture for about 80 metres, then zig-zag down to a stile and footbridge at the bottom.

The footbridge is rather narrow and partly constructed from sections of railway line, but there is a comforting handrail to assist progress. Once over, continue directly ahead across a grassy meadow to reach a waymarker on the far side and here bear slightly right to a stile, then follow the winding footpath through trees to reach a further stile that gives access to the bed of the old Carmarthen to Cardigan **railway line**. Turn right along this and follow it for approximately 3km, passing through two gates en-route, with lovely views over the river and surrounding woodlands.

The line was authorised in 1854 as the **Carmarthen and Cardigan Railway's** abortive attempt to create a rail link between the two towns. By 1860 the Company managed to construct the line as far as Conwil before having to cease further works until it could raise enough capital to build the line to Pencader in 1864. The line was extended to Landysul a few months later but by that time the Company was in severe financial difficulties and went into receivership. In 1867 attempts were made to run the line using horse drawn buses along the uncompleted sections but in 1881 the Company was wound up. The line was then acquired by the Great Western Railway who managed to complete the line as far as Newcastle Emlyn in 1898 but, despite its name, that was as far is it ever went. Instead, the link to Cardigan was achieved by the Whitland & Cardigan Railway, which followed a route to the west.

Pixie's Ears fungi growing on a fallen tree in the Tyweli valley

Just before reaching the new road, a fence prevents further progress along the track bed, but bear left onto a footpath alongside a fence that leads to a junction with a road. Turn right along the road, crossing the new road bridge into **Pont-Tyweli** and at a junction by the Half Moon Inn, bear right back to the river bridge and retrace your steps back into New Road, but instead of following the footpath round the river, continue along New Road back to the car park.

CASTLES, GARDENS AND FORESTS

Paxton's Tower (Walk 6)

WALK 5

Brechfa Forest West

Start/Finish	Keepers Lodge picnic site and car park, Brechfa Forest (SN 522 319)
Distance	14km (9 miles)
Ascent	340m (1110ft)
Time	4–5hrs
Maps	Explorer 186
Refreshments	None
Public transport	None to the start of the walk. Closest services are bus 282 Carmarthen–Brechfa or bus 283 Carmarthen–Brechfa–Llandeilo. Services run daily but are infrequent.

Brechfa Forest is one of the best-kept secrets in southwest Wales. This beautiful region of mountains and forests, cared for by Forestry Commission Wales, covers some 6500ha and is criss-crossed by numerous forestry roads, tracks and footpaths, most of which are well surfaced, making it an ideal winter venue when many of the mountain and lowland trails are little more than a bog. Despite its fairly easy access, being just a few kilometres northeast of Carmarthen, the forest is virtually devoid of people, bar the very occasional mountain biker or horse rider. Please remember, Brechfa is a working forest and occasionally tracks may have to be closed for safety reasons when felling is being carried out, so take heed of any warning signs.

From **Keepers Lodge** picnic area, go left on a broad track, passing a large storage barn on the right and descending gently into the forest, eventually swinging left over the Afon Marlais to a T-junction with another broad track. Turn right along this, climbing steadily along the sides of the **Afon Marlais**, with occasional glimpses of the miniature river down to the right and crossing small tributary streams that tumble down from the wooded hillside to the left. After 2.5km, the track swings gently round to the left and runs parallel with the contour lines for a while before continuing its gradual ascent up the valley. ◄

As you climb, you are likely to see buzzards and kites circling overhead, as well as all the common woodland species, and some less common ones such as crossbill and goshawk.

At a track junction, alongside a recently cleared area of forest, take the narrower track to the right which continues to climb, now more steeply up the side of the Afon Marlais, with the open moorland of **Mynydd Llanfihangel-rhos-y-corn** across the valley to the right. The track eventually leaves the forest, levels out and reaches a narrow, moorland road near the ancient site of **Crug-y-Beow**. The change in scenery here is quite a contrast from the confines of the forest, with grassy moorland covering the summits of the nearby hills and with far reaching views back over the forest towards the Brecon Beacons.

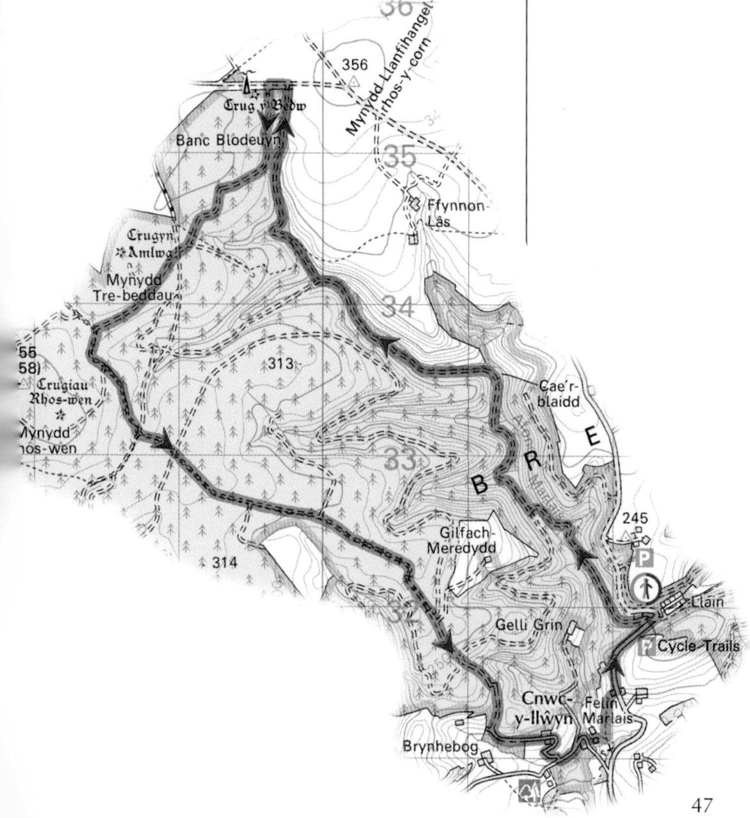

THE FOREST OF GLYNCOTHI

The forests of the Afon Cothi, in the early Middle Ages, were heavily wooded, forming the Forest of Glyncothi, a source of fuel, building materials, game, honey and nuts. It was also vital to the defence and independence of the Welsh principality of Deheubarth, in which the forest stood, forming a formidable barrier to the heavily armoured, mounted knights of the Norman kings and their Marcher lords who had been attempting to subdue Wales from the 11th century onwards. Following the final subjugation of Wales by Edward I in 1283, Glyncothi became a Royal Forest administered under the harsh Forest Law and overseen by the king's foresters. Forest law involved severe punishment for offences against 'venison' and 'vert', or 'greenery' and included trees, coppices, the underwood and feeding ground of the game. Unlike today, when venison means deer, in medieval Glyncothi it was an all embracing term for all forest animals, including red, fallow and roe deer, wild boar, hare, marten, fox and wolf. Forest Law was finally abolished in 1640, with most of the ancient oak forest being felled and cleared by the late 17th century.

Turn left along the road, going left again after 200 metres and joining a broad forest access road that heads

Banc-y-Daren across the Afon Cothi from Brechfa Forest

The flower strewn footpath leading to Bryn Marlais

back into the forest. Keep straight ahead, ignoring a broad track off to the left to reach a crossroads and go straight over onto a much narrower track, where the blades of wind turbines soon come into view and pierce the skyline above Mynydd Rhos-wen directly ahead. Proceed to another crossroads of tracks, where the right hand track is little more than a grassy break through the trees and here go left, heading downhill between trees on a stony track to reach a major crossroads. Go straight over, now on a broad forest road that rises gently at first before levelling out and going straight on over at another crossroads and beginning a long, steady descent through the forest.

Pass through a gateway by a rough parking area and join a narrow, poorly surfaced lane that descends more steeply, with pleasant views ahead across the Cothi Valley towards Banc-y-Daren. The lane eventually exits the forest and passes between cottages at **Cnwc-y-llŵyn**, the first sign of habitation on the whole walk, before winding down between fields to a T-junction. Turn left for 200 metres, negotiating a sharp right hand bend alongside buildings at **Felin Marlais**, then go immediately left over the **Afon Marlais** and into a farmyard. Bear slightly right between farm buildings, joining a rough track that climbs steeply, soon swinging round to the left and up to a road junction at Bryn Marlais. This last section is a delight in spring, with the banks awash with bluebells, the track bed a swathe of wild garlic and the trees alive with birds that are busy trying to feed their newly hatched chicks. Turn left along the road and walk back to the car park at Keepers Lodge.

WALK 6

National Botanic Garden and Paxton's Tower

Start/Finish	National Botanic Garden of Wales (SN 518 178)
Distance	11km (7 miles)
Ascent	295m (965ft)
Time	3–4hrs
Maps	Explorer 186
Refreshments	Café at the National Botanic Garden; pub in Llanarthne
Public transport	Bus 279 Carmarthen–Llandeilo. Very restricted services run Mon–Wed and Sat.

This magnificent walk provides the chance to explore one of Carmarthenshire's and Wales's finest attractions, the National Botanic Gardens of Wales, with its Great Glasshouse, the largest single spanning glasshouse in the world. The walk then heads roughly northeast, using quiet lanes and clearly marked footpaths to the village of Llanarthne before climbing through woodland to the striking folly of Paxton's Tower, a noted landmark throughout the Tywi Valley.

▸ From the car park of the **National Botanic Garden**, return to the main entrance and turn right along the cycle-way, skirting the car park and grounds of the gardens, before bearing left along its service road to a T-junction. Turn left then first right along the Nantgaredig road to just beyond buildings at Erwlas, then go right along the access drive to **Wern Farm**, turning immediately left through the farmyard, past farm buildings and through a concrete parking bay, for farm machinery, to a kissing gate in the far right hand corner which gives access to a field. Walk over the brow of the field to another kissing gate and on in the same direction down another field to reach a lane.

The garden is open April–Sept 10am–6pm; Oct–March 10am–4.30pm.

Bear right along the lane for almost 1km to where it turns sharply right and here continue directly ahead along the drive to Greenhill Farm. Where the access drive swings left, go through the kissing gate directly ahead

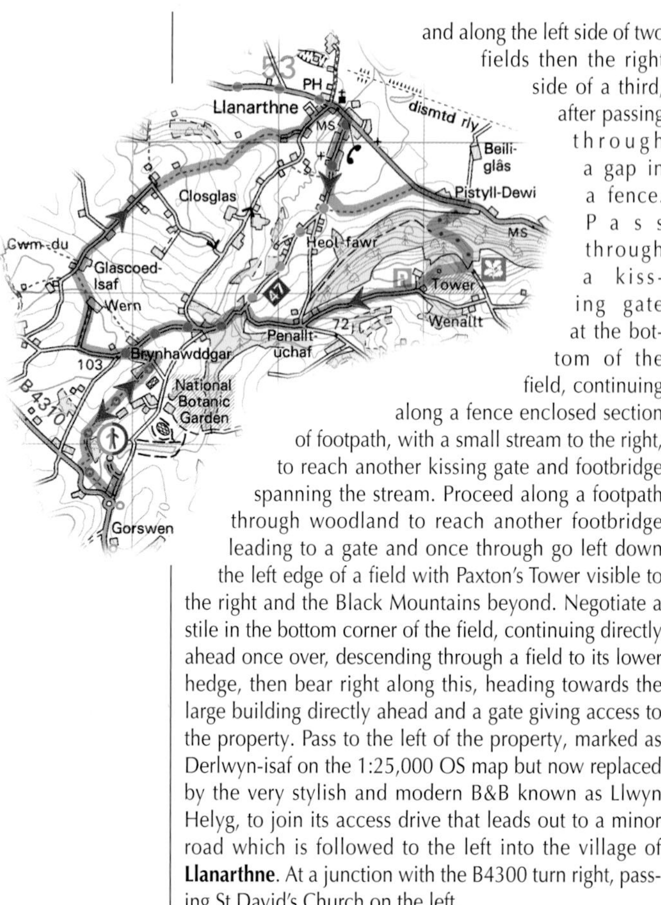

and along the left side of two fields then the right side of a third, after passing through a gap in a fence. Pass through a kissing gate at the bottom of the field, continuing along a fence enclosed section of footpath, with a small stream to the right, to reach another kissing gate and footbridge spanning the stream. Proceed along a footpath through woodland to reach another footbridge leading to a gate and once through go left down the left edge of a field with Paxton's Tower visible to the right and the Black Mountains beyond. Negotiate a stile in the bottom corner of the field, continuing directly ahead once over, descending through a field to its lower hedge, then bear right along this, heading towards the large building directly ahead and a gate giving access to the property. Pass to the left of the property, marked as Derlwyn-isaf on the 1:25,000 OS map but now replaced by the very stylish and modern B&B known as Llwyn Helyg, to join its access drive that leads out to a minor road which is followed to the left into the village of **Llanarthne**. At a junction with the B4300 turn right, passing St David's Church on the left.

The origins of **St David's Church** date back to the sixth century when it was dedicated to St Arthney. In the late and early 11th century a new church was constructed on the site, this time dedicated to St David and originally lime washed, creating a very distinctive landmark.

Quiet lanes around Llanarthne

On reaching the Emlyn Arms, turn right opposite the **pub** along a lane signposted to Paxton's Tower, passing several houses on the way and 50 metres beyond the Llanarthne village sign, go left over a stile into a field and bear half right across this, heading for a gateway some 80 metres left of the diagonally opposite field corner. Go through the gateway, walk along the left edge of the next two fields, with the ruins of Dryslwyn Castle directly ahead, to a kissing gate leading into the adjacent field and go right along this to reach the B4300. Turn right along the road, passing **Pistyll Dewi Farm**. ▸ Some 200 metres beyond the farm, go right onto a broad track that climbs steeply through the woods, swinging sharp left part way, before the woodland on the left gives way to open pasture. Some 50 metres beyond this point there are two gates, one on either side of the track. Go through the right hand one and immediately bear left up a steep, sloping pasture with **Paxton's Tower** soon coming into view.

The farm is named after a spring called Pistyll Dewi located high in the adjacent wooded hillside and dedicated to Dewi Sant (St David).

Sometimes known as Nelson's Tower, **Paxton's Tower** was built by William Paxton to commemorate the death of Lord Nelson at the Battle of Trafalgar in 1805. The striking folly has overlooked the Tywi Valley for over 200 years and the views from its lofty position are quite outstanding. The first floor served as a banqueting room which can still be accessed via a narrow staircase, the second floor consisted of an apartment designed for a prospect room, while an upper chamber housed panels of coloured glass depicting the life of Lord Nelson which are now on display in Carmarthen Museum.

After visiting the tower, pass through the kissing gate in the surrounding fence and bear right along a faint grassy track leading to a kissing gate that gives access to a quiet lane and go right along this, past the parking area for the tower with the dome of the glasshouse at the Botanic Garden clearly visible ahead. Descend steadily to reach a crossroads, continue straight on, still descending to a T-junction then turn left, passing an attractive picnic area on the side of the Afon Gwynon, a tributary

Paxton's Tower projects above the Allt Pistyll-Dewi

Amazing views along the Afon Tywi from Paxton's Tower

of the Afon Tywi. The road now begins to ascend out of the valley, passing the North East Lodge of the former Middleton Estate, before turning left along the Botanic Gardens service road once more and retracing your footsteps back to the start.

The **National Botanic Garden of Wales**, created on the former grounds of Middleton Hall, was the brain child of William Wilkins of Carreg Cennen, Trapp. He first heard about the Middleton Hall estate from his aunt who told him of the archaeological remains that she had seen there, and, after visiting, he too was very impressed by the quality of the surviving ruins and their aesthetic value. With a great deal of enthusiasm and effort, Wilkins succeeded in getting the idea of the garden implemented and it was officially opened on 20 July 2000 by HRH the Prince of Wales.

WALK 7

Dryslwyn, Aberglasney and Golden Grove

Start/Finish	Car park at Dryslwyn Castle (SN 552 203)
Distance	14km (9 miles)
Ascent	210m (695ft)
Time	4–5hrs
Maps	Explorer 186
Refreshments	Tearooms at Aberglasney
Public transport	Bus 279 Carmarthen–Llandeilo stops at Golden Grove. Very restricted services run Mon–Wed and Sat.

Due to the fact that this walk is mainly on quiet country lanes, good tracks and reasonable footpaths, it's a good option for winter days, when many of the county's public rights of way are ankle deep in mud. Having said that, it's a most enjoyable and varied outing at any time of year as it crosses the attractive Afon Tywi twice, climbs up through Golden Grove, the old estate village to a large mansion, passes the magnificent gardens at Aberglasney, which are open all year, and offers the walker the chance to explore the ruins of Dryslwyn Castle.

The ruins of **Dryslwyn Castle** dominate the settlement of Dryslwyn, itself little more than a few scattered houses set around a crossroads in the Tywi Valley. This and Dinefwr Castle, near Llandeilo, occupy a place of great affection in the minds of the Welsh people as they are forever associated with the princes of Deheubarth, the ancient kingship of southwest Wales. In 1287, Rhys ap Maredudd, the lord of the castle, rose in revolt against Edward I of England over a land dispute. The latter sent an army of 11,000 troops who besieged the castle, undermining its walls and pounding them with a huge siege engine until part of them fell. The castle then remained in English hands until the early 15th century when it was mostly demolished.

Dryslwyn Castle

From the car park beneath the castle, with its picnic benches and lovely views along the Tywi Valley, go left along the road towards the hamlet of **Dryslwyn**, taking the first turning on the right past isolated cottages and farms to reach a road junction. Keep right along the no through road for 800 metres, to just before farm buildings at Alltygaer where a waymarked gate on the left gives access to a field. Turn right along the bottom of the field to its right hand hedge and bear left alongside it, climbing to a stile in the top corner and once over bear slightly left to pass through a gate in a fence. Climb steeply to a stile, bearing right once over, on a narrow footpath that runs along the edge of woodland, and after crossing a footbridge spanning a small stream, keep left into a sloping field, ignoring a rough track that runs off to the right, to reach a stile on the far side. The footpath now becomes more distinct as it climbs steadily through woodland to reach another stile and, once over, continue along the bottom edge of a sloping field followed by a long, narrow field to eventually join a rough field track. Pass through two gateways and onto a surfaced lane with runs past the entrance to **Aberglasney Gardens**.

A GARDEN FOR ALL SEASONS

The origins of the house and its gardens are shrouded in obscurity, and even though recent research has uncovered some of the mysteries and myths, much is still to be unearthed. For more than four centuries, the fortunes of Aberglasney and its various owners have followed a rollercoaster ride, sometimes reaching splendid heights and at other times swooping down into the depths of debt and decay. By 1955, much of the house was in a sad state of decay and the magnificent gardens were choked with weeds. The fortunes of Aberglasney changed, however, following a series of sales when the estate was split up and a number of tenant farmers acquired land they had previously rented. When the house portico was offered for sale by Christie's, the law intervened as its removal from a listed building constituted an offence. A prosecution followed and the publicity that ensued raised the profile of Aberglasney, to the point where a small band of enthusiasts of historic houses and gardens formed and set about procuring the property. The remaining estate was sold to the Aberglasney Restoration Trust in 1995 and by 1999, Aberglasney was open to the public.

At a T-junction just beyond the entrance to the gardens, bear right for 50 metres then go left into the quiet village of **Llangathen**, taking the first turning on the right, which is a no through road that leads towards the church.

The **church** is dedicated to St Cathen, believed to have been King of Dyfed and Brecon sometime in the late seventh century. The tower is of 13th-century construction and there are three medieval family chapels inside. The 'beadstead' memorial to Bishop Rudd is one of the finest of its type in Wales.

After visiting, walk round the church, passing through a gate on the eastern side of the church yard onto a lane and go right along this and down to a road junction. Turn left along the road, which descends through woodland initially before crossing the Afon Tywi, then continue between fields which do flood in the wetter months of the year, to a junction with the B4300. Go straight over and climb steadily into the hamlet of **Golden Grove**.

Walk up through the hamlet until the entrance to Golden Grove Country Park is reached on the left and here turn right, along a quiet lane, for 300 metres to just before the road crosses a stream and go left, through an iron kissing gate, into a sloping meadow. Climb up through the meadow to a stile at the top and proceed along the footpath, which zigzags steeply up through woodland, following the line of a narrow but steep gorge with a stream in the bottom. At the end of the woods,

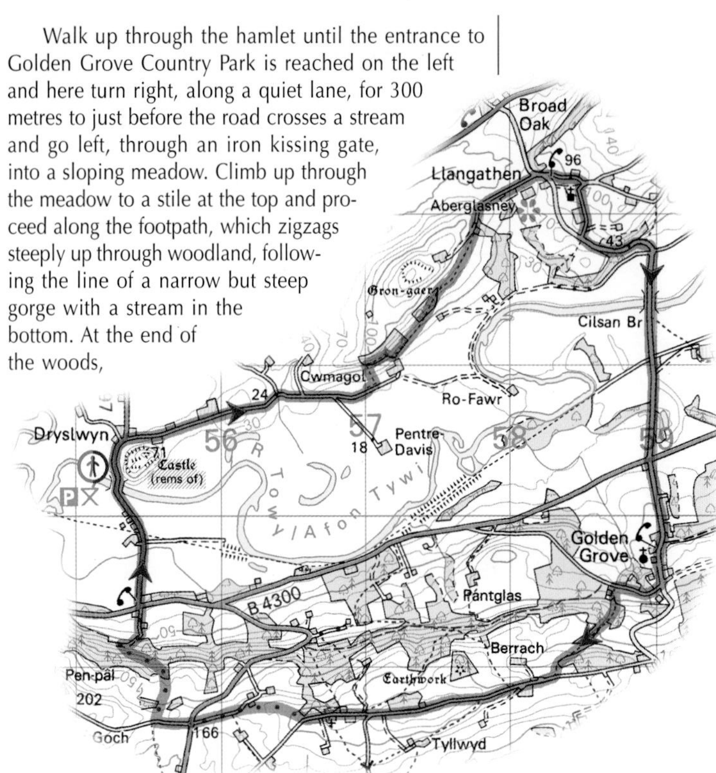

climb a stile into a pony paddock, bear diagonally right to the far top corner where there is a stile beside a gate. Once over, follow a rough track into a field, continuing along its right edge to a junction with a lane and go right, following the lane for 3km and enjoy far reaching views across the rolling Carmarthenshire countryside.

About 200 metres after passing a small **chapel** on the left, and just before the lane swings round to the left, turn right onto a rough track that is used by farm vehicles to access fields on either side. At a junction with

Llangathen church

the B4297, go straight across onto another narrow lane, following this for 300 metres before turning right down a rough track, opposite a footpath sign and kissing gate, and which zigzags steeply down through woodland. At a junction with the **B4300**, cross straight over onto the B4297, crossing the Afon Tywi once more before returning to the car park at **Dryslwyn Castle**.

WALK 8

Llandeilo and Dinefwr Park

Start/Finish	Main car park off Crescent Rd, Llandeilo (SN 630 223)
Distance	8km (5 miles)
Ascent	175m (575ft)
Time	2½–3hrs
Maps	Explorer 186
Refreshments	All kinds in Llandeilo; café in Dinefwr Park
Public transport	Trains from Swansea and Llanelli. Bus 280 Carmarthen–Llandovery. No services on Sun.

This most enjoyable outing is based around the attractive town of Llandeilo and the National Trust's Dinefwr Park. Besides having an interesting geology, along with superb flora and fauna, Dinefwr Park boasts two Roman forts, a medieval castle (once the seat of the Welsh kings and princes of Deheubarth), two medieval townships of Dinefwr and Newton and the post medieval mansion of Newton House.

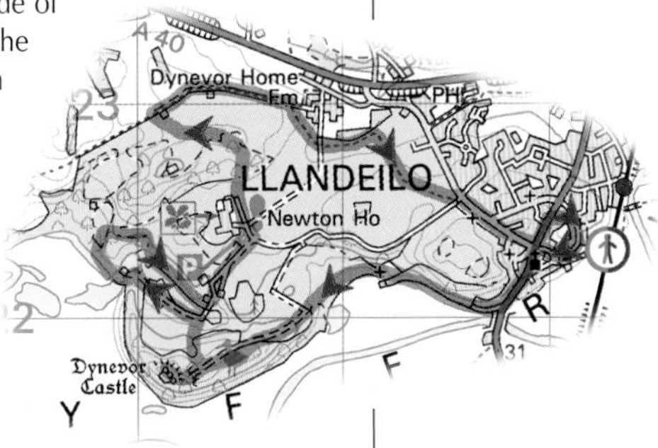

From the top right hand side of the car park, pass beneath the archway by an information board to enter the main street through Llandeilo (the main A483 road), and go left along it, passing numerous shops, cafés, restaurants and pubs. At the far end of the town, pass St Teilo's Church on the left and proceed along Bridge Street, heading downhill towards **Llandeilo Bridge**, but just before the bridge, veer right past a row of terraced cottages, on a lane that soon becomes a rough track.

St Teilo was a sixth-century contemporary of St David, whom both the church and town are named after. By the sixth century Llandeilo had become a very powerful and prosperous religious authority and the seat of the Bishops of Teilo. It's possible that there was a crossing over the Afon Tywi at this point as early as Roman times, and the existence of Roman forts at nearby Carmarthen, Llandovery and Dinefwr Park, which would have been joined by road, would tend to support that view. Before the construction of the present bridge, in 1848, a former medieval stone bridge was located a short distance downstream.

Pass through the right hand one of a pair of gates to enter **Dynefwr Country Park Castle Woods Nature Reserve**, cared for by the Wildlife Trust of South West Wales, and join a broad track leading through the reserve.

The **woods** are of national importance for invertebrates that inhabit dead wood, many of which are very rare. During spring, flowers such as dogs mercury, primrose and wood anemone cover the woodland floor, to be replaced by bluebells in late spring and early summer which carpet the floor beneath a canopy of oak, ash, beech and sycamore.

At a fork in the track, alongside an information board describing the local bats, bear left and descend to the abandoned church, passing to the rear of the building before walking past the church porch and continuing down to go through a gate on the far side of the churchyard. Turn immediately right alongside the wall of the churchyard to negotiate a second gate, then bear left along the bottom edge of a sloping field, passing through two gates in quick succession at the far end, to re-enter Castle Wood.

A narrow path now climbs steadily through the woods before entering a large, open meadow in Dinefwr Country Park, where the footpath continues in the same

The abandoned church in Dinefwr Country Park

direction before going left, along a track, which soon takes you back into woodland. There are good views over the parkland and the towers and turrets of Newton House from the track, which soon leads round to the splendid ruins of **Dinefwr Castle**.

Dinefwr Castle dates mainly from the 13th and 14th centuries, but its general structure was dramatically altered in the 17th century when it was converted into a 'romantic' ruin. Even at first glimpse, it is obvious that the long ridge on which the castle stands is a position of extraordinary defensive strength. Because of this, it is highly likely that defensive settlements occupied this site long before Dinefwr was built, but to date no evidence has been

> unearthed to support this notion. Dinefwr, along with its neighbour, Dryslwyn, are of major importance, not only in the immediate vicinity but in the minds and traditions of the Welsh people. Both sites now stand among the most treasured monuments of the Middle Ages to be found anywhere in Wales.

After enjoying the ruins and the magnificent views from its battlements, retrace your steps along the track for 300 metres to reach a bench on the left, then go left, on a gravelled footpath leading down through the woods, before continuing in the same direction through a sloping field. Pass through a gateway on the far side, leading into Bog Wood and follow a track that passes one of several ornamental lakes, to where the path forks at the end of the lake. Bear right above the old pump house, now fully restored and operated during the summer months, pass through a gate and walk back along the opposite side of the lake which soon crosses a series of boardwalks that

Superb views from Dinefwr Castle

Reflections and the boardwalk in Bog Wood

take you dry shod over various wet and boggy areas. At a junction in the boardwalk go left, past several carved benches, eventually passing through a gate onto a track and go left, climbing steadily past a series of buildings. Walk past the main car park and refreshment booth, following the 'Visitor Route' towards **Newton House** and passing to the right of this splendid building.

> 'New' Dinefwr, or **Newton House** as it is now known, is thought to date back to 1603, with the corner towers and cupolas being added in the 18th century. The whole building was refaced in limestone between 1856 and 1858. Lord Dinefwr sold the castle and the estate in the late 1970s, after which it fell into disrepair until being taken over by the National Trust in 1990.

Go through an iron gate, now with the lovely, open expanses of Dinefwr Park to the right and continue onto a wooden gate giving access to woodland. Once through, proceed along a broad track, following signs for the 'Tree Walk', passing first the old ice house, followed by the deer enclosure, both on the left, to eventually pass through a set of double gates. Continue along the broad track, which swings round to the right, passing a house known as Pen Parc, to reach a waymarker and iron kissing gate on the right.

This leads onto a field track, which is followed for 20 metres before veering left, now on a grassy footpath along the edge of the field, with super views ahead over the western fringes of the Black Mountains. At the bottom of the field, negotiate a pedestrian gate, cross a drive, then walk around the edge of a field, with woodland to the left, eventually veering right around the edge of a pond to join a footpath between fields. After 10 metres, turn sharp right through a kissing gate, walk along a footpath that runs over the brow of a field and swings gently left towards houses in **Llandeilo**. Turn left along the main access drive to Dinefwr Country Park, then right on reaching the road, which is followed for 200 metres before going right into Carmarthen Street.

In post medieval times, **Carmarthen Street** was an important commercial centre with many of the buildings having stone, vaulted cellars beneath them where stock was kept. The building on the right, facing the old Market Hall, was built in the 1850s and used to be the National School. At the end of Carmarthen Street is Rhosmaen Street, where the majority of Llandeilo's commercial outlets can be found today, along with most of its refreshment stops.

Cross straight over into Abbey Terrace, turning left at the end back into Crescent Road, which is followed to the left, back to the main car park.

THE CAMBRIANS OF CARMARTHENSHIRE

Nant Hirgwm near Clynsaer Farm (Walk 11)

WALK 9

Dolaucothi

Start/Finish	Dolaucothi Gold Mines Car Park (SN 662 403)
Distance	11km (7 miles)
Ascent	410m (1345ft)
Time	3–4hrs
Maps	Explorer 186 and 187
Refreshments	Pub and café at Pumsaint; pub in Caio
Public transport	Buses 288/289 Llandovery–Lampeter. Infrequent services on Mon, Tue, Thu and Fri only.

This spectacular walk, in the heart of the picturesque Cothi Valley, is littered with fabulous views, historic sites, contrasting countryside and extensive wildlife. Based around the wider Dolaucothi Estate, a once thriving estate with extensive parkland, now managed by the National Trust, the route visits the pretty little village of Caio, wanders through the conifer plantation of Caio Forest, then traverses high pasture before returning through the Cothi Valley back to Dolaucothi. The estate and the adjacent Roman Goldmines are both now visitor attractions.

From the car park at **Dolaucothi Goldmines**, go left for 40 metres to reach the crossroads and here turn left again, climbing quite steeply on the road to Caio, with good views down over the goldmine complex.

Goldmining on this site dates from Roman times, although it's possible that some panning for gold in the Afon Cothi could have occurred as early as the Bronze Age. Following the Roman departure from Britain in the fifth century, the mines were abandoned and lay forgotten for centuries, until a modest revival was undertaken in the 19th and early 20th centuries. However, the mines were abandoned again in 1938 due to flooding and poor returns. Between 1975 and 2000, the mines were subjected to extensive archaeological and mining research by students from Cardiff University School of Engineering, and it was during this time that the Roman origins of the mines was realised, along with the extent of the operations carried out by the Romans. Features from those early days can still be seen in places, particularly the water supply system for the mine, which involved building a series of leets, tanks and aqueducts, the longest of these being 11km.

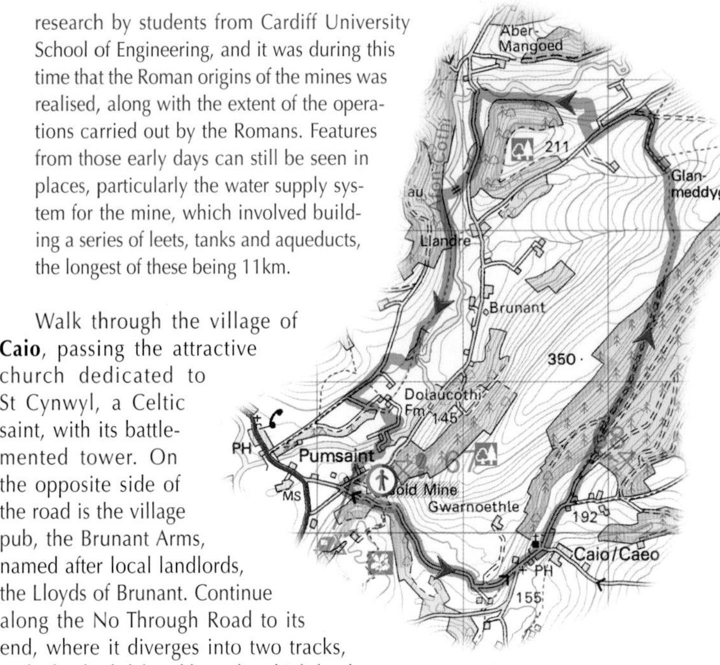

Walk through the village of **Caio**, passing the attractive church dedicated to St Cynwyl, a Celtic saint, with its battlemented tower. On the opposite side of the road is the village pub, the Brunant Arms, named after local landlords, the Lloyds of Brunant. Continue along the No Through Road to its end, where it diverges into two tracks, and take the left hand branch, which leads to a parking area on the edge of Caeo Forest.

This is a large **conifer plantation**, established over unenclosed moorland and consisting of Douglas Fir, Norway Spruce and Larch, among others. Alongside the forest tracks, where light penetration is increased, moorland plants such as heather and bilberry grow.

Immediately beside a Caeo Forest sign, before reaching the parking area, bear left down a track and keep left at the bottom to cross a footbridge over the tiny Afon Annell, with a picnic bench and BBQ area on the opposite side. Where the track forks, bear left, climbing up through the forest and keeping directly ahead where

The village of Caio

the main branch swings sharply left, now on a slightly narrower track that continues to climb through tall walls of conifer, eventually emerging from the forest at a gate with the most magnificent views over the Cambrian Mountains.

Pass through the gate, continuing in the same direction across the top corner of a field to negotiate another gate on the far side, still proceeding in the same direction along a rough track that follows the fence line. Go through a third gate and begin the gentle descent towards buildings at **Glan-meddyg**, passing in front of barns and the farm house to join the main access track which is followed out to a minor road. Turn left along the road, climbing a stile on the right, beside a gate after 400 metres, to join a new footpath. ◂ Walk along the right edge of a field to a second stile, bearing right on the opposite side along the line of an old field boundary and continue following the hedgeline all the way round the field to reach a stile beneath northern flanks of the shapely, tree crowned hill of Allt Dinbeth. Once over, contour across the next field to a gate on the far side, just above the **Afon Cothi**, and join a rough field track, with

This footpath is not shown on the current OS map.

the river babbling away to the right. Pass through another gate, proceeding in the same direction along the top of a steep field bank for 40 metres, then turn sharp right down into the lower part of the field and bear left to a stile leading onto a lane beside a bridge spanning the river.

The **Afon Cothi** is an important spawning ground for trout and salmon and consequently a favoured river for sports fishermen. The fish swim upstream to lay their eggs in the abundant gravel beds of the river, some 32km from its confluence with the Afon Tywi and 44km from the sea in Cardigan Bay.

Turn left along the lane for about 500 metres, to a stile on the right with forest access gates immediately to the left. Climb the stile and make a steep descent down to the river, then turn right to a metal footbridge spanning the Cothi alongside a ford. ▶ Once over, bear right to climb a stile beside a gate, proceeding up a rough, steep track for 50 metres to reach a waymarker and turn left on a footpath through woodland. On exiting from the woods, follow an obvious track through fields, furnished with frequent red waymarkers, to just before **Dolaucothi Farm** where a footpath sign points to the right along the edge of a field. At the end of the field, bear left to a stile leading onto a track and turn left along this to reach a track heading off to the left towards Dolaucothi Farm B&B.

This footpath is also not shown on current OS maps.

The old **Dolaucothi mansion** is still evident in Dolaucothi Farm, which occupies what was the mansion's northern wing. In 1679 it contained six hearths and was described as 'simple and dignified'. By 1871, the house had reached quite large proportions, being in the form of a cube with 28 rooms and a five bay, three-storey front, with the older parts of the house behind. Much of the house fell into disrepair in the 1900s and the Johnes family donated it to the National Trust in 1941. It now comprises 2500 acres, which includes the

Caoi church tower appears above the trees

farmhouse, goldmines, parkland and a large upland farming estate with nine tenant farmers and 24 tenant cottages.

Follow the track to where it forks, then bear right, still following signs for the B&B for a further 50 metres, veering right, off the track, onto a well surfaced footpath through woodland to reach a stile leading into a field. Bear left through the field, with Dolaucothi Farm to the left, to a second stile leading onto a footpath alongside the old walled garden, followed by a third stile giving access to a track. Turn right, now with the river to the left, to cross a bridge spanning the river, first constructed in 1836 and rebuilt in 1956 following flood damage, and on the far side follow a broad track to gate and stile on the right. Climb it, continuing along a pleasant footpath through woodland and initially above the river to reach the road directly opposite the start.

WALK 10

Cil-y-cwm

Start/Finish	On the road outside St Michael's Church, Cil-y-cwm (SN 753 400)
Distance	13km (8 miles)
Ascent	390m (1280ft)
Time	4–5hrs
Maps	Explorer 187
Refreshments	Neuadd Fawr Inn, Cil-y-cwm
Public transport	None

This outstanding walk starts out from the charming village of Cil-y-cwm, nestling in the upper reaches of the Afon Tywi Valley, an area criss-crossed by an extensive network of footpaths and bridleways and untouched by the ravages of industry. Besides the tranquil meadows and fields in the immediate vicinity of the village, to the west and north lie the uplands of the Mynydd Mallaen, an expansive area of low mountains that once served as the refuge of the Princes of Deheubarth during the wars with the Anglo-Norman invaders. As one would expect in such a diverse landscape, a wealth of habitats exist, supporting a vast array of flora and fauna, particularly birdlife. This walk traverses sections of high moorland, where footpaths are faint or nonexistent in places, and should only be attempted in good weather or if proficient with a map and compass.

From **St Michael's Church**, which is well worth visiting either before or after the walk, cross the main road running through the village, walk along a surfaced alleyway opposite, that runs between cottages and past the chapel, to reach an iron gate giving access to a field. Traverse this and the next two fields, climbing stiles at their boundary junctions, then bear diagonally right through a fourth field, heading towards the summit of Pen Lifau, directly ahead. Climb a stile on the far side, walk along the edge of a narrow pasture, negotiating a stile and footbridge on the far side, join an old boardwalk leading into a very rough, wooded pasture, bearing diagonally right through this to reach a stile in the far corner. Once over, bear slightly left through two more similarly vegetated pastures, now with super views to the left towards the Carmarthen Fan, to reach a stile beside an iron gate, turning right on the far side, alongside a stream to a lane.

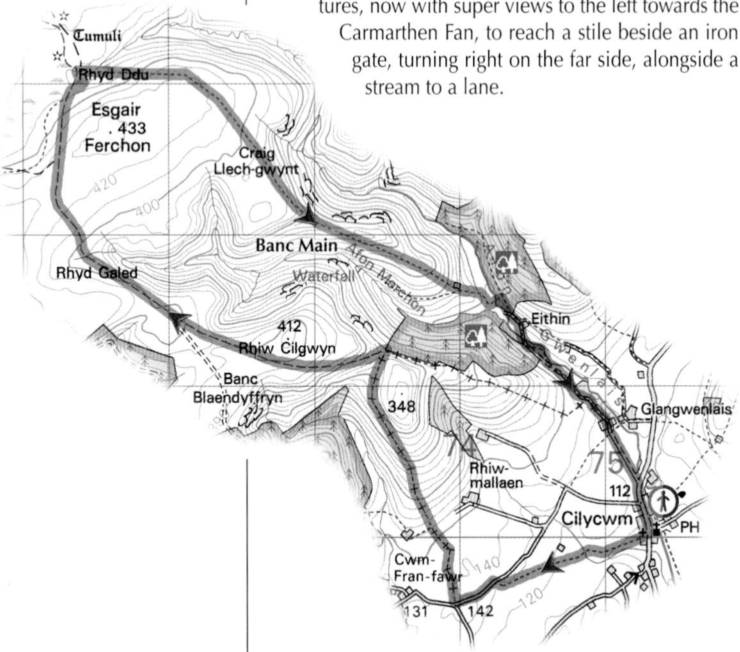

Burial cairns and standing stones raised by **Bronze Age** people to commemorate their dead are still visible on the surrounding hills, providing evidence that the area around Cil-y-cwm has been settled for over 5000 years. There are also outlines of several Iron Age hill forts.

Turn left along the lane to a T-junction, where the way ahead is rightwards, over a stile and along a broad track for 300 metres to a stile on the right. Once over, continue along a rough track hemmed in between a fence on the right and an old field boundary on the

The Nant Fran

left, and soon beginning a steady climb onto the lonely expanses of the Mynydd Mallaen. The track eventually levels out, as it contours along the sides of the Nant Fran Valley, eventually swinging gently rightwards and climbing again, through a series of gates at a sheep-penning area, to reach a junction of paths and tracks on the col, overlooking Cwm Merchon to the north. Turn sharp left onto an initially indistinct footpath that rises steadily along the southern flanks of **Rhiw Cilgwyn**, with ever improving views over the surrounding countryside and into the Brecon Beacons.

On the expansive hill of **Mynydd Mallaen** it is unlikely that you will see another soul but, although it feels like a fairly remote area, you will not be alone. Flocks of mountain sheep graze these rough hillsides, while red kites, peregrines and

The scant remains of Cwm-Merchon

buzzards make use of the up draughts from the valleys as they gracefully soar above the woods and hills. The clunking call of ravens is frequently heard, often well before you spot them, and skylarks are common too, their melodious song filling the air in spring and summer. Ringed plover, merlin and ring ouzel also nest on these wild, wind blown hills.

The path begins to level off as it passes the rounded top of Rhiw Cilgwyn and becomes much more obvious after being joined by a track from the left, finally crossing a ford over the infant **Afon Merchon**. Eventually, the path crosses the ridge known as **Esgair Ferchon**, now giving expansive views to the west towards Ceredigion, and 40 metres after this, at a crossroads of tracks, go right, avoiding the descent towards the forest in the Cothi Valley ahead. The track now becomes much more difficult to follow, as there are several faint tracks across this part of the hill, but keep contouring round to the right, avoiding the descent into a shallow valley to the left, soon to head directly eastward, back over the ridge.

As soon as the ridge begins to slope back down to the east, bear diagonally right, now in a southeasterly direction where a slightly better footpath cum sheep trod materializes and runs along the broad ridge between the Afon Gwenlais to the north and Afon Merchon to the south. After walking for just under a kilometre in this direction, it is necessary to bear slightly left, now in an east-south-east direction, heading for the twin rocky outcrops at **Banc Main**, now on a much more distinct footpath that descends quite steeply for a while. After crossing the craggy outcrops, the path descends very steeply down the ridge to a stile, alongside the ruins of Cwm-Merchon, to re-enter enclosed pasture. Once over the stile, keep ahead along a low brow that descends into **Afon Gwenlais**, cross a footbridge over the river and join a track that passes to the right of a house.

Keep on along the track until opposite the lovely old farmhouse at Penstacan and bear right, following the surfaced track out to the road, which is then followed to the right for the short walk back into **Cil-y-cwm**, or to give it its full name, Llanfihangel-yng-Nghilycwm (St Michael's in the Secluded Vale).

In the 16th century, **Cil-y-cwm** became an important point on one of the main droving routes between Wales and England and the cobbled gutters, still visible along the sides of the main street, were used to feed animals gathered here on their journey to towns and cities over the border. In the 18th and early 19th centuries, at the height of the droving business, the village had no less than nine hostelries.

WALK 11

Cynghordy

Start/Finish	Esgar-fwyog car park on the western edge of the Crychan Forest (SN 837 412)
Distance	10.5km (6½ miles)
Ascent	360m (1180ft)
Time	3–4hrs
Maps	Explorer 187
Refreshments	None on route
Public transport	Bus X14 Carmarthen–Builth Wells. Services on Fri only.

This fine, varied walk encounters dark pine forest, open moorland, a tranquil river valley, quiet lanes and farmland. It feels quite remote at times, despite the fact that it encounters two of the main transport networks through this part of Wales, spends a good section along the valley of the Afon Brân and passes close to several farms. Cynghordy Viaduct is the highlight of the route, being 846ft long, with a continuous series of 18 arches that carry the Heart of Wales Railway high across the valley. If you can time your walk with one of several 'nostalgia' days, watching the steam trains chug across the viaduct, billowing steam and smoke as they run between Swansea and Shrewsbury, is a fine sight to behold.

Crychan Forest and neighbouring Halfway Forests, once the property of Forestry Commission Wales, are now under the stewardship of Natural Resources Wales who have created kilometres of waymarked trails to cater for walkers, horse riders, cyclists and carriage drivers. The forest is situated in lovely countryside between the Brecon Beacons and the Cambrian Mountains, an area criss-crossed with old tracks and drovers roads, once used to drive livestock through the wild mountains of Mid Wales to Smithfield Market in London. No longer will you hear the bleating of sheep, the lowing of cattle or the shout of the drovers, more likely the mew of buzzards and red kite as they soar above the green canopy on thermals of rising air. There is a good contrast of trees in the forest, ranging from the native oak, ash, beech and hazel of the original ancient forest to the tall, stately, imported conifers.

From the car park, walk back to the road, bearing left along it for 200 metres before turning right along a bridleway which soon swings left as it descends into the forest. ▸ After 300 metres, in the bottom of a shallow depression, go sharp right along a narrower footpath that descends quite steeply before crossing a broad forest track onto the continuation footpath on the opposite side. Immediately before the path swings right, to run along the edge of a field at the bottom of the slope, bear sharp left onto another footpath, now passing beneath deciduous trees rather than pines. The footpath follows the boundary between forest and field, eventually reaching a metal pedestrian gate on the right that gives access to a field that is crossed to a broad track on the far side. Bear left along this, fording the pretty **Nant Hirgwm**, which could be a boots and socks off job during the wetter months, and continue alongside the stream for a further 50 metres to reach a metal gate leading onto an enclosed track. Go through another gate in front of **Clynsaer Farm**, turn left once through, past the farmhouse and proceed along its access drive to reach the A483.

The current OS map shows the bridleway as plummeting straight down through the forest, whereas the extant route zigzags its way down into the Nant Hirgwm.

Cross the road with care, bear left along it for 40 metres to a pedestrian gate on the right, leading into a field and turn left along its left

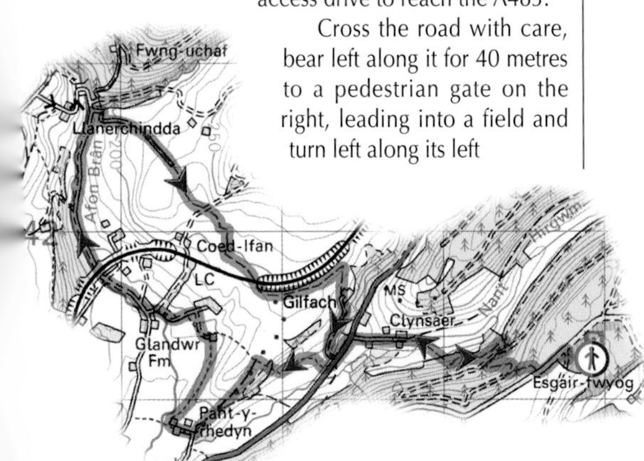

Fine views over the Cambrians from Crychan Forest

edge to reach a gate giving access to a farm track. Go right along the track, which is the access drive to Gilfach Farm and the way of the return leg, but after crossing the bridge over a stream, turn left into a field then go immediately right, ascending a hill alongside a fence on the left. Where the fence line swings left, keep left alongside it to eventually reach a gate at the very far end of the field and once through, turn sharp right and ascend another field, climbing alongside a cut and laid hedge towards a copse of trees. On reaching the wood, the definitive footpath continues on alongside the hedge, but this is extremely steep, so it is best to veer left for 40 metres then zigzag up through the trees to reach a kissing gate through the top fence and 50 metres left of the top right hand corner of the field.

Once through the kissing gate bear slightly left, passing alongside the communications mast and continue alongside the right hand hedge line to reach a gate. Go through the gate, bear left past the scant remains of the former Pen-y-bryn Farm and proceed along a hedge-lined track, with Cynghordy Viaduct coming into view in the distance to the right. The track descends steadily to a junction, where the surface becomes metalled, and here bear right along the access drive to **Pant-y-rhedyn Farm**, continuing through the farmyard to the first metal gate on the right. Once through, pass beside an old barrel-roofed barn onto a rough track through a field, go through a gateway on the far side, continuing in the same direction through the next two fields, eventually bearing slightly left and heading towards buildings at Clynboidy, directly ahead.

The name **Cynghordy** means 'meeting house' in English, but despite having all the elements that one would expect in a village, including a church, pub, post office, station and chapel, these elements are so widely scattered along the valley that there is no sense of a nucleus to the community. Nevertheless, the houses, farms and buildings are set in delightful countryside.

Some 100 metres before reaching Clynboidy, veer left towards a series of gates leading onto the access drive to the farm and follow this towards buildings at Treffolied Farm, negotiating a gate in front of the farm before turning left down its access drive. At a junction with a minor road turn right to reach Cynghordy Chapel and the **viaduct**.

Cynghordy Viaduct, 846ft long, Grade II listed, described as one of the finest railway monuments in Wales, is impressive. It carries the affectionately known Heart of Wales Railway Line high above the valley of the Afon Brân. It is a rather elegant structure, curving gently and rising slightly as spans the valley via a series of 18 arches, each having an individual span of 102ft, with a maximum height above the valley floor of 109ft. Prior to its construction, along with the nearby 2998ft-long Sugar Loaf tunnel, the 19km stretch between Llandovery

The elegant and mightily impressive Cynghordy Viaduct

in the south and Llanwrtyd Wells in the north was the only missing section in the completion of the Central Wales Line, linking Swansea to Shrewsbury and it presented the railway engineers with a severe challenge. It was eventually built by the Llanelli Railway and Docks Company, with construction beginning on 22 March 1867 and the first train successfully traversing the span on 12 May 1868. It was an important feat of engineering at the time, linking the industrial towns of Swansea and Llanelli with those of Liverpool, Manchester and other large industrial regions of England.

Pass beneath the viaduct, continuing along the road with the **Afon Brân** for company to the left until immediately before the road crosses a tributary stream and here go right, along a bridleway to the right of the stream. Pass through a gate, following a rough track that climbs steadily out of the valley to where it swings right, into a field, and here proceed directly ahead, following the right hand hedge line, now on a less distinct track that is largely obscured by rushes. Keep alongside the hedge, passing through three gates to eventually follow a more distinct, stony track, now with open views to the right over the Brecon Beacons and along the Tywi Valley. Pass through a fourth gateway, keeping on in the same direction, now with a fence to the left initially, but where a gate gives access to the field on the left, veer rightwards along a more distinct track, now with a fence to the right once more. The track soon begins to descend, swinging gently rightwards as it does so and passing through a gateway to reach a junction of tracks. Proceed directly ahead over a small stream, walk along the right side of a rough pasture to cross a second stream, continuing on through the next pasture, now heading for the obvious, yellow emergency phone alongside the railway line.

Cross the line, heeding the clear warning notice, and once over go left along the edge of two fields, following the course of the **railway line**, now with the distinct, conical shape of Sugar Loaf directly ahead. At the end of the second field turn right, down a track, pass through the farmyard at **Gilfach Farm**, continuing on its access drive to eventually rejoin the outward route, just in front of the A483, and retrace your steps back to the car park.

WALK 12

Llandovery

Start/Finish	Castle car park, Llandovery (SN 767 342)
Distance	5.5km (3½ miles)
Ascent	55m (185ft)
Time	2hrs
Maps	Explorer 187
Refreshments	All kinds in Llandovery
Public transport	Trains on the Mid Wales Swansea–Shrewsbury line. Bus 280 Carmarthen–Llandovery; services infrequent, none Sun.

This is a short but very enjoyable circular walk that explores a large part of Llandovery and some of the attractive countryside to the north of the town, including a lovely return leg alongside the Afon Tywi. It is well worth carrying binoculars on this walk as a wide variety of wildlife can be seen, especially alongside the river.

The name of **Llandovery** is derived from its geographical position on the banks of the least significant waterway that flows around it, the Afon Dyfri, now known as the Bawddwr. Four rivers flow through, or around, Llandovery: the Tywi, Gwydderig, Brân and the Bawddwr, the latter being diverted during medieval times to act as a kind of moat around the castle, but also as an open sewer for the occupants. Bawddwr was a rather apt name at the time as it means 'dirty water' in English. It was put into a culvert beneath a road in 1836.

From the car park, walk past the Heritage and Information Centre, a very informative place to linger if time allows, to reach Kings Road, the main A40 road through the town, and go right along it. After passing the King's Arms Hotel on the left and just before the bridge, spanning the Afon Brân, bear left off the road, passing a row of terraced cottages to reach a footpath sign and go left along it, with the river to the right. At the end of the footpath, bear right on a track, still with the river to the right, but where the track rises to enter a field, keep left along a footpath to the rear of houses and on reaching a stile on the right, ignore it by turning left between houses. Turn right along a road, which soon swings round to the left, but where it swings round to the left for a second time, go straight ahead on a footpath, to the right of a children's play area and onto reach the A483 road. Cross with care to enter a minor road opposite, that climbs steadily, away from Llandovery to reach **St Mary's Church** on the right, built on the site of the old Roman Fort of Llandovery.

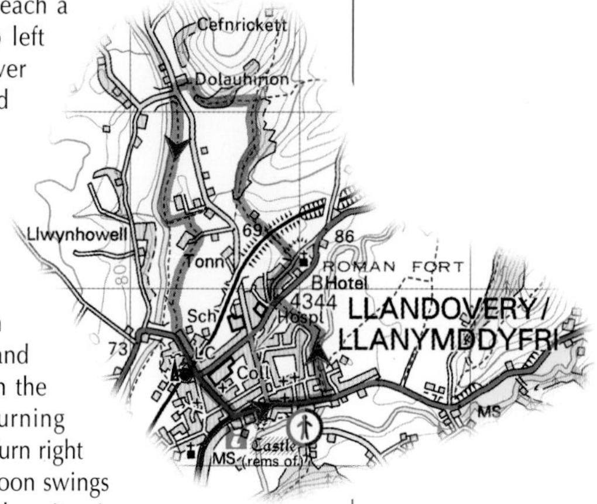

The **Roman fort of Alabum** was established on this very spot. The Romans saw Llandovery as being an important place from which to control traffic passing along or across the Tywi Valley, and so by around AD50 they built the fort and a Roman Road from here to the next Roman Fort at Pumsaint. A small town evolved around Alabum, but following the fall of the Roman Empire, and the withdrawal of the Roman Legions from Britain, the town declined and was eventually abandoned.

St Mary's Church, Llanfair-ar-y-bryn, or translated into English St Mary's on the hill, is a medieval building of the Anglican denomination. The eastern part of the church is probably 13th century, as it has windows dated to that period, with bricks from the old Roman fort being partly used in the

Llewelyn ap Gruffyd, staunch supporter of Owain Glyndwr, stands watch over Llandovery

construction of the east wall; an early example of reclamation.

Directly opposite the church, climb a stile on the left, into a field and descend to its bottom left hand corner where a pair of stiles gives access to a flight of steps leading up to the **Central Wales Railway Line**.

The **railway** reached Llandovery in 1858, an extension from Llandeilo of the Vale of Towy Railway from Llanelli and the industrial regions in the south of the county. The London and North Western Railway reached Landovery in 1868 from Craven Arms in Shropshire, creating a continuous line through Mid Wales to England. The coming of the railway was not good news for all however, as it signalled the death knell for both the Drovers' trade and the mail coaches, both of which used Llandovery as an important resting point on the turnpike road between South West Wales and England, now the A40.

Cross the line, descend steps on the opposite side into a field, bearing left across this to its far left hand corner to climb another stile. Once over, swing slightly rightwards across a second field, climb a stile on the far side, then bear right across a farm track to another stile. Now proceed between a wooded bank on the right and a stream on the left, eventually crossing the stream via a footbridge, but continue in the same direction for 50 metres to climb a stile on the left into a field. Walk along the right edge of the field, climbing a stile just left of a field gate at the far end, turn left along the bottom of the next field, soon joining a rough field track and where this forks, take the upper level to reach a stile beside a gate. Once over, proceed for a further 20 metres, then bear left through a field, climb a stile, cross an access drive to reach a lane and bear left along this for a short distance before turning right, along the lane leading to Siloh and **Pont Dolauhirion**. ▸

There has been a bridge here, spanning the Tywi, since medieval times, with mention of a timber structure, the 'bridge of Dolhir', in records dating from 1396.

Do not cross the bridge, but go left over a stile and join the delightful riverside footpath through a series of meadows beside the Afon Tywi. After passing through the third kissing gate, it is now necessary to divert away from the river, due to erosion of the footpath, by bearing diagonally left, across the bottom corner of a field to another kissing gate. Once through, go left alongside a stream, cross a lane, turn immediately right over a footbridge, then walk along the right edge of a field to cross another lane into a second field. Proceed along its right edge, passing an agricultural feed packing plant, go through another kissing gate, then bear slightly right across the next field to reach yet another kissing gate, positioned between two old, corrugated iron, sheds. Now follow an enclosed grassy track, climb a stile beside a field gate, proceeding along the left edge of the next two fields,

Llandovery

eventually joining a grassy track that leads to the **A40**, just left of Pont Gadwyn Chain Bridge on the outskirts of Llandovery. Go left along the A40 and back to the car park.

THE HIGH MOUNTAINS OF Y MYNYDD DU

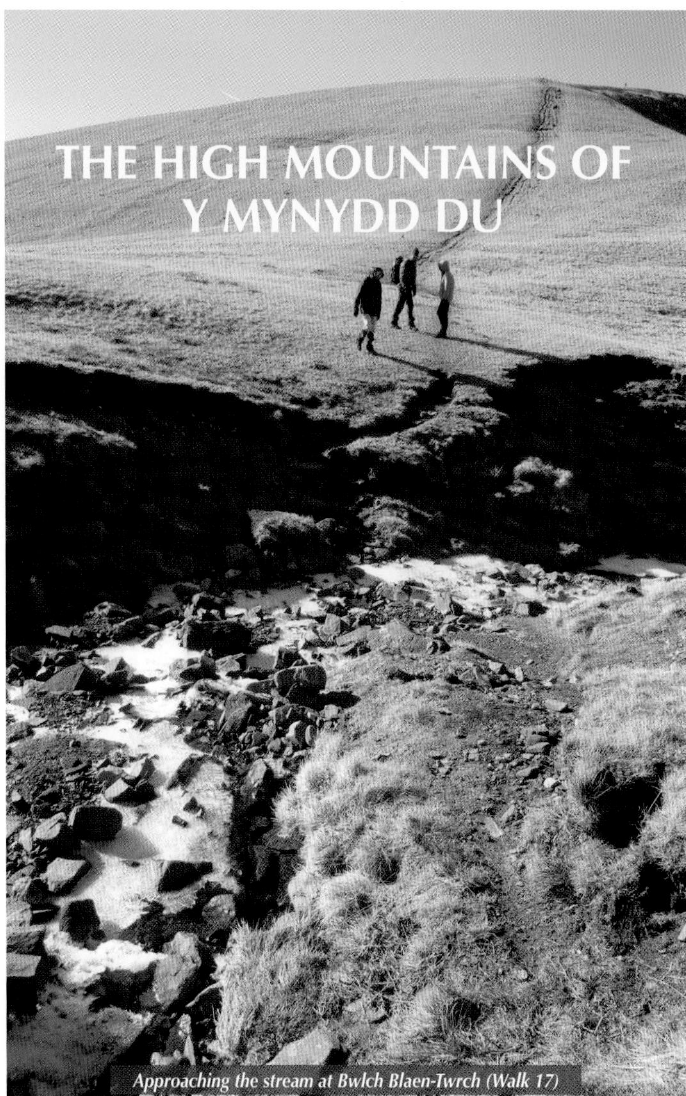

Approaching the stream at Bwlch Blaen-Twrch (Walk 17)

WALK 13

Mynydd Myddfai

Start/Finish	Myddfai Visitor Centre car park (SN 772 301)
Distance	11km (7 miles)
Ascent	385m (1265ft)
Time	3–4hrs
Maps	Outdoor Leisure 12
Refreshments	Café at start
Public transport	None. Taxi from Llandovery.

This is an exhilarating walk that climbs steadily from the lovely village of Myddfai, once renowned across Wales (see below), following in the footsteps of the ancient physicians up onto the remote, windswept heights of Mynydd Myddfai. The walk along the ridge affords splendid views over the Usk Reservoir towards the Carmarthen Fan and on into the heart of the Brecon Beacons. This section of the walk follows some fairly indistinct footpaths and should not be attempted in poor visibility unless well versed in the use of a compass. The return journey follows a very quiet no-through road, past isolated farms with hedgerows bright with wild flowers and alive with butterflies and song birds in spring and summer.

Myddfai Community Hall and Visitor Centre is a delightful place from which to start this walk as it gives a wealth of information about the village and its history, much of which can be digested with a delicious cake and coffee before you set off. The centre was officially opened by Their Royal Highnesses, The Prince of Wales and Duchess of Cornwall, on 30 June 2011.

From the Visitor Centre, turn right along the road, bearing right opposite St Michael's Church along the road towards Llanddeusaint, but taking the first road on the left after 100 metres, which gives a chance to view the day's objective, Mynydd Myddfai across the fields to the left. This quiet lane climbs steadily for just over 1.5km to reach buildings at **Sarnau** where the road swings round to the right and here leave the tarmacadam for a bridleway directly ahead, signposted to the 'Physicians Well'.

The bridleway continues to ascend, but now more steeply between hedges and trees, before swinging left and breaking out into open countryside on the south-western flanks of Mynydd Myddfai with fine views to the right over the Black Mountains. Proceed along the initially obvious sunken track, again signposted to the Physicians Well, but when it becomes less obvious as it runs through tall grasses and rushes, keep on in the same direction, climbing gently to the rim of a shallow valley where a fence is reached with a gate and stile leading into open access land. Once through, bear half right on a fairly clear footpath come sheep trod, soon passing above a spring, the Physicians Well and crossing the tail end of old stone excavations.

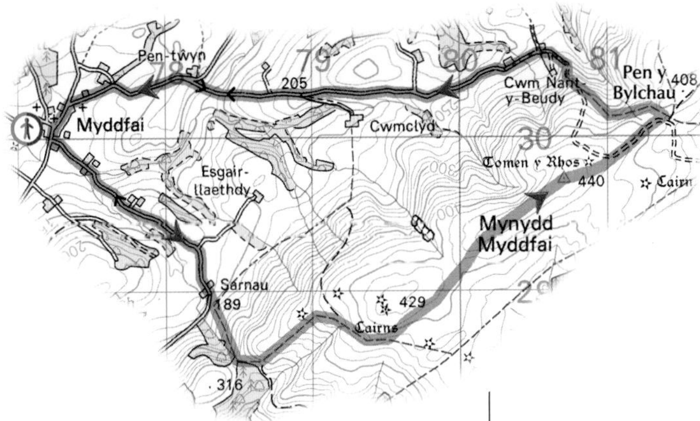

The **Physicians Well** is so called because it was from here that water with healing properties was collected by the Physicians of Myddfai, along with various medicinal and herbal plants from the area, in order to treat their patients. Legend has it that the Lady of the Lake at Llyn y

A fingerpost points the way to the Physicians Well

Fan Fach had three sons, Cadwgan, Gruffydd and Einion. She taught them how to recognise and use medicinal herbs and they and their children became renowned for their expertise. In truth, the first of the physicians was Rhiwallon, court physician to Rhys Gryg, Lord of Dinefwr Castle around 1200. He was granted land in Myddfai, so becoming known as the Physician of Myddfai, from where he treated the poor for free.

Immediately beyond the stone workings, bear left off the main footpath onto a subsidiary footpath that climbs steadily towards the ridge ahead. Within 250m, the path intersects a deep ditch (more remnants of stone workings) that runs along the line of the ridge in a northeast - southwest direction and here turn left and follow the line of the ditch as it climbs towards the summit of **Mynydd Myddfai**, again with splendid views to the east over Glasfynydd Forest and into the high peaks of the Brecon Beacons.

> **Mynydd Myddfai** lies at the very western end of the Brecon Beacons National Park and Fforest Fawr Geopark, forming a long ridge aligned southwest to northeast with a number of distinct tops separated by shallow cols. The hill is composed of different rock formations, mainly sandstones and mudstones, but the prize for the quarry men of old is the narrow band of flaggy micaceous sandstones, known as the Tilestones Formation, which was extracted for roof tiles and which the visible line of excavations follows. Along with the old quarry workings, there are several ancient cairns on the hill and a variety of Roman remains can be found on Mynydd Bach Trecastell, just to the northeast of the main summit.

Where the mine workings peter out, continue on a good quadbike track along the crest of the ridge, climbing almost imperceptibly to the summit trig point at 440m (1445ft) where there is a magnificent 360° panorama. From the trig point, continue on in the same direction, soon passing a cairn on the right where old excavations are visible again and just beyond here, the grassy track bears right to join a much broader track which again runs in a northeasterly direction, descending slightly to a col and watershed at **Pen y Bylchau**. A few metres before the stream and ford at the col, bear hard left along an indistinct path around the top of rushes, but which soon joins a better quadbike track that runs along the western slopes of Cwm yr Olchfa. As the track descends it becomes more distinct, passing a few boggy sections where springs surface, eventually zigzagging down steep slopes to reach a stile beside an iron field gate that marks the boundary of open access land.

Climb the stile and follow an enclosed track that soon swings left past farm buildings at Bwlch Brân, then becomes surfaced near the attractive buildings at **Cwm Nant-y-Beudy**. Continue along this very pleasant

Mynydd Myddfai from Myddfai village

hedge-lined lane, with the slopes of Mynydd Myddfai to the left. Today, very few of the medicinal herbs that made Myddfai famous can be found in the surrounding fields, but the hedgerows are still quite bountiful, with yarrow, primrose, foxglove, betony and lesser celandine being fairly common. Along with the wild flowers come the insects, particularly butterflies that flit from flower to flower and who accompany you as you make the return to the village of **Myddfai** after approximately 3km.

WALK 14

Usk Reservoir

Start/Finish	Parking area at the southern end of the dam wall (SN 833 286)
Distance	8km (5 miles)
Ascent	125m (405ft)
Time	2–3hrs
Maps	Outdoor Leisure 12
Refreshments	None
Public transport	None

This is an easy stroll around one of the most remote, yet beautiful reservoirs in Wales. Much of the walk follows broad forest trails through the Glasfynydd Forest, which wraps around large parts of the reservoir, so a good walk for very hot days when respite from the sun is a requirement or on windy days, when the tall pines offer shelter from the worst of the gusts. However, having said that, the forest is not so dense that it hides the local scenery, because there are some wonderful views to be enjoyed of the broad escarpment of the Carmarthen Fan to the south, westwards towards the giants of the Brecon Beacons and northwards across Mynydd Bach Trecastell.

From the parking area, follow the surfaced access road across the top of the dam, crossing the sluice over which flows the infant **River Usk**, with lovely views to the north over Mynydd Bach Trecastell with its Roman camps and ancient standing stones. On the far side of the dam bear left along a surfaced road, walking past the launch and landing point on the left where several sailing dinghies are usually hauled up on the shore of the reservoir. Continue along the road, passing an isolated house on the right. ▸

Looking back from this point into the heart of the Brecon Beacons, Pen y Fan and Corn Du can be seen on the far horizon, while Fan Frynach and Fforest Fach occupy the middle distance.

At a fork in the track, just before a water tower projecting from the reservoir, leave the surfaced road by bearing right onto a broad forestry track with a pedestrian gate alongside a locked metal barrier. At a second fork, 100 metres further on, veer left onto a lower track just

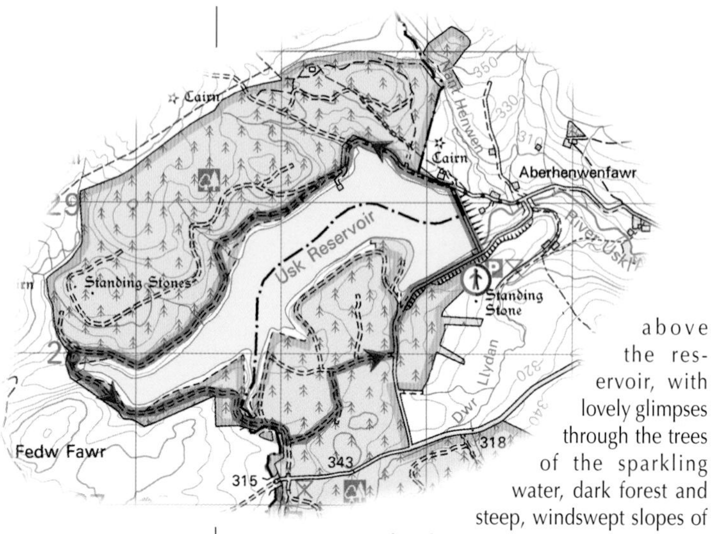

above the reservoir, with lovely glimpses through the trees of the sparkling water, dark forest and steep, windswept slopes of the Black Mountain.

Usk Reservoir is situated at an altitude of 300m (985ft) above sea level and cradled between the remote uplands of Mynydd Myddfai and Mynydd Wysg. The reservoir is the most recent one to be built in the Brecon Beacons National Park with excavation and building starting in 1950. The inaugural ceremony, attended by Her Majesty the Queen, took place on the 6 August 1955. The reservoir covers some 280 acres and holds 2,700,000,000 gallons of water when full, part of which flows out of the eastern end as a continuation of the River Usk, while the rest of it can be used to satiate the thirst of people and industries in Swansea.

At the far end of the reservoir the track forks, just before the fence that marks the boundary to open access land, and here bear left towards a ford on the Afon Sgio. Splash through the water if you wish, but by turning left just before the ford, a path leads to an attractive wooden footbridge that gives a dry shod crossing of the stream with a picnic bench just to its left. ▶

This is a good halfway point for lunch or a little light refreshment with superb views over the Black Mountains.

Once over the bridge, bear left along a track that climbs steadily through a much denser area of forest before swinging right, away from the reservoir, to reach another footbridge, this time spanning the River Usk as it flows into the reservoir.

Plenty of **wildlife** inhabits the coniferous economic forest. If you are completing this walk during the months of May and June, you may see the lovely marsh fritillary butterfly with its orange, yellow and dark brown mosaic wing pattern. It is also a popular hunting ground for red kite, most often seen drifting

Fabulous views over Usk Reservoir towards the Carmarthen Fan

Semi-wild ponies grazing around Usk Reservoir

lazily overhead. In this area, you will see that parts of the forest have been felled and partly replanted.

Go left on the far side of the bridge, climbing over a low bank before descending to a junction of tracks where the route goes sharp left along a stony track. If you were to continue directly ahead for 200 metres at this point, the road and parking area is reached at Pont'ar Wysg. At a T-junction with a broad forest track go left and at another junction, continue directly ahead, beginning a gentle descent to a metal barrier and the reservoir access road which is followed to the left and back to the car park.

WALK 15

Carn Goch and the Afon Sawdde

Start/Finish	Car park on minor road south of Bethlehem, near Carn Goch Iron Age hill fort (SN 641 242)
Distance	15km (9½ miles); shortcut 9.5km (6 miles)
Ascent	350m (1150ft); shortcut 275m (900ft)
Time	5–6hrs; shortcut 3–4hrs
Maps	Outdoor Leisure 12
Refreshments	None
Public transport	None

This magnificent walk on the fringes of the Brecon Beacons has a lovely mix of open moorland, forest, a deep cut river gorge and very quiet country lanes, along with one of the largest and most impressive Iron Age hill forts in Wales. This walk should really be undertaken on a fine day when the variety of scenery can best be appreciated and when time allows to explore the megaliths. Despite its length, it is not particularly strenuous and is mostly on clear paths, field tracks, lanes or forestry roads, but be warned, in winter months sections of the walk can be extremely wet, which may be of interest if you intend to enter the local bog snorkelling championships. There is also a shorter alternative to the main walk, which is outlined in the route description.

From the car park, join the grassy footpath to the left of the information panel, soon swinging right alongside an oak tree, with views over the Tywi Valley already starting to open out. Cross the first hill, occupied by the remains of the smaller of the two hill forts on this site, **Y Gaer Fach**, descend into a shallow depression between the two hills, then climb steadily uphill towards **Carn Goch**, passing through the remains of the fort's walls, into the main site of **Y Gaer Fawr**.

Translated as the 'red cairn', **Carn Goch** is the largest Iron Age hill fort in Wales and even today it is very impressive; in prehistoric Wales it must have been a site to behold. It is also very much about location, being constructed 675ft (206m) above the Tywi Valley, on a hilltop whose presence dominates the surrounding countryside and offers unparalleled views. The ready supply of sandstone on the hill allowed the Iron Age builders to construct not just one, but two hill forts here, known appropriately and respectively as Y Gaer Fach (the small fort) and Y Gaer Fawr (the large fort). They occupy two separate summits on the same long ridge and the geographical descriptions, implicit in the names, really allow you to easily identify which is which.

Walk through the huge enclosure, passing through a gap in the remains of the ramparts on its northeastern side, bearing right once through and descending to a minor road. Turn left along the road, following it to a sharp left hand bend, just beyond a cattle grid, and here continue directly ahead, on the left and lower of two tracks, heading into woodland. Immediately

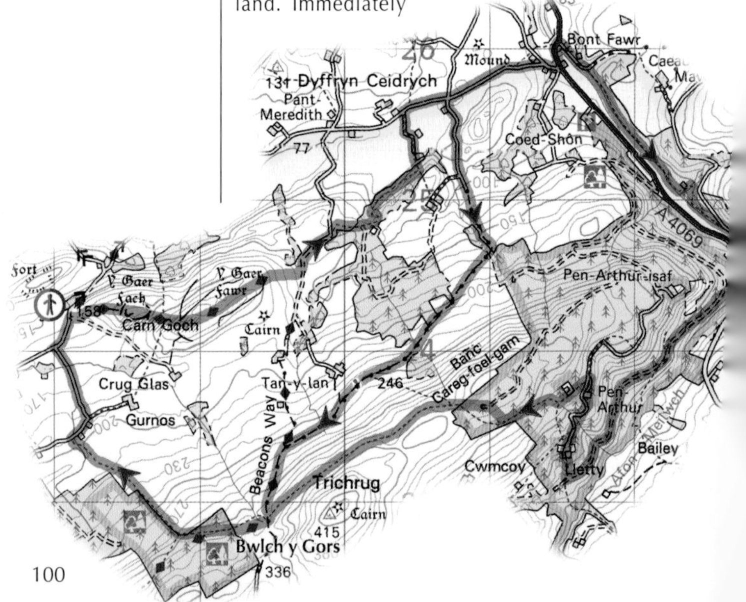

Standing stone on the approach to Carn Goch

before a field gate, after 50 metres, turn right onto a wall enclosed footpath to reach another gate giving access to Talylan Wood and once through, go left along a woodland track.

Talylan Wood is privately owned but walkers are welcome, provided they adhere to the well-marked footpath. The wood was purchased as it is a very special and sensitive site for growing mushrooms, with 25 different species being found in its confines.

Immediately alongside the double gates leading to Red Pig Farm, go left onto a grassy footpath that descends through the trees, climbing two robust stiles en route, before level walking ensues on a pleasant, grassy footpath along the bottom edge of the woods. Immediately before an iron pedestrian gate, with no public access, climb the ladder stile over the wall on the left, then walk through the middle of a grassy meadow which is a mass of buttercups, purple clover, yellow rattle and many other wild flowers in the summer months. Climb a stile on the opposite side, turn sharp right to a second stile, leading onto a farm access drive, and turn left along this, passing the site of a Roman villa at Llysbrychan en route. On reaching a lane turn right.

Shortcut

For a shorter alternative, go right along the lane for 350 metres, turning right at a crossroads and along a surfaced lane. Where this forks, keep left, climbing steadily on a rough track along the edge of fields, passing through numerous gates and crossing several streams, to eventually reach a T-junction with another track and a Brecons Way footpath sign. Turn left up this to rejoin the main walk at **Bwlch y Gors**.

Walk along this quiet lane, eventually reaching a junction with the **A4069**, follow this to the left for 200 metres then, immediately after crossing the bridge over the river, turn sharp right along a surfaced lane that runs parallel with river. Where the track forks, keep left, passing buildings and crossing a small stream, to join a forestry track above the pretty gorge of the Afon Sawdde.

The **Afon Sawdde** is a popular river with wild water canoeists, it being narrow, fast and with several sections of rapids and white water, particularly after rain. The river flows for 18km from its source at Llyn y fan Fach, the lovely glacial lake beneath the Carmarthen Fan in the Brecon Beacons, before confluencing with the Tywi near Llangadog. For large sections of its length, it has cut deep into the underlying bedrock, exposing the Devonian and Silurian rock sequences, resulting in parts of the river being designated as a geological Site of Special Scientific Interest.

Where the track ends, go left on a narrow footpath, heading away from the river and round the back of a ruined building and over a shallow gully. Turn right by a waymarker, along a narrow footpath that crosses a footbridge over the Ffinnant stream, before swinging rightwards to eventually join a minor road. At a T-junction go right over the main river, go right again along the A4069, turning left after 100 metres, immediately alongside Coopers Cottage, to join a narrow, stony footpath that climbs steadily into Pen Arthur Forest. At a junction with a broad forest road turn left along it, climbing steadily for quite some distance before flattening out and crossing two streams, which are rather more heard than seen.

After rounding a sharp right hand bend in the road, proceed for a further 330 metres, then turn very sharp right (no signage) onto a footpath that runs parallel to the road, in the direction you have just travelled, and climbing steeply for 70 metres before swinging left to pass through an area devoid of trees. The footpath soon passes to the left of the isolated buildings at **Lletty**, then follows its access drive out to the right to just before buildings at **Pen Arthur** and immediately opposite a stile giving access to that property, turn left along a broad, grassy fire break (waymarker) that leads to a large vehicle turning circle. Walk straight across this to join the continuation footpath on the opposite side, soon reaching the edge of the forest at **Banc Careg-foel-gam** (the Rock of the Bare

The gushing Afon Sawdde

hill), the highest point on the walk at 350 metres, with magnificent views back over Carn Goch, the Tywi Valley and into Mid Wales.

Turn left along the perimeter fence, passing through a gate after 100 metres, keep left to a stile, then join the waymarked footpath below Pen y Bicws, now with views along the valley to Dinefwr Castle and Dryslwn further along. Stay on the track for a little over 1.5km to a junction with a broad track, furnished with a Brecons Way footpath sign, go straight over to a stile 50 metres ahead. This area is aptly known as **Bwlch y Gors** (the Pass of the Marsh) and after wet weather can be virtually impassable, so, to outflank it, go left along the broad track for 200 metres to the next gateway and turn right, on a narrower track that returns you to the dry(ish) side of the stile. In dryer conditions, climb the stile and bear right along a stony track to a gateway after 15 metres, then veer left across the top of a field, passing a superbly situated, but most unlikely positioned, bench.

In the far left corner of the field, pass the end of a drystone wall, turn right between the wall and a fence to a stile giving access to Carreglwyd woodland and follow a narrow footpath that forms part of Beacons Way. The path is level at first, but soon descends steeply to a broad track and here turn right to a gate. Once through, turn immediately left to climb a stile, then veer right into the open field before turning left and walking roughly 5 metres right of the left hand field fence to avoiding walking down the course of a stream bed. Walk through three fields in this way, eventually climbing a stile and crossing a footbridge into an open pasture, covered with rushes and walk straight across the middle of this, and on in the same direction down a sloping meadow to a stile, 20 metres left of the bottom right hand corner. Once over, bear diagonally left through another rush covered, ever narrowing meadow to a gate, then walk through a long, narrow pasture with the Nant Cwm-du stream to the left. At the far end of this, pass through a gate, left of a cottage, to join a minor road and turn right along this back to the start.

WALK 16

Carreg Cennen Castle

Start/Finish	Car park at Carreg Cennen Castle (SN 666 193)
Distance	6.5km (4 miles)
Ascent	230m (765ft)
Time	2–2½hrs
Maps	Explorer 165 and 186
Refreshments	Café at Castle Farm
Public transport	None

Short but energetic, this well-signed walk takes in the western fringes of the Mynydd Du (the Black Mountain), where the brooding, yet majestic ruins of Carreg Cennen Castle dominate the surrounding countryside. Perched on a precipitous limestone cliff, the castle ruins are visible, from various angles, for much of the walk. Besides the castle, the walk enjoys superb views over the adjacent mountains and surrounding countryside, visits the source of the Loughor, crosses the lovely River Cennen twice before following an exquisite footpath through woodland to reach the castle entrance.

From the car park, walk into the farmyard at Castle Farm, but immediately before the first building on the right, go right through a small courtyard, through a gate into a field and head down this to its far left hand corner where a kissing gate leads onto a lane. Turn left, ignoring the first footpath sign on the right, to descend quite steeply round a left hand bend to reach a second footpath sign immediately before the attractive buildings at Pantyffynnont. Go right here, through a gate and down a sloping field to negotiate a stile in the bottom right hand corner. Ignore the stile immediately right but take the steep, narrow path that descends to a stile at the bottom of the slope and once over bear half left to a footbridge spanning the **River Cennen**.

On the far side of the footbridge, bear diagonally left and head uphill to climb a stile in the top corner of the field, then climb steeply along a slightly sunken footpath towards farm buildings directly ahead. Just before the buildings veer right for 70 metres, pass through a hedge gap then bear right along a farm track to eventually ford the **River Loughor**. ◂ On the opposite side, continue along the track which swings round to the left, to a stile, on the left after 150 metres and once over, walk along the right edge of a field, following the course of a rough track and crossing a footbridge over a stream, to a stile left of a gate. Climb this and bear slightly right along a sunken track, which doubles up as a stream bed in wet weather, then cross a more open area before walking alongside the infant River Loughor to another stile beside a gate.

Usually little more than a shallow stream during the summer months but after heavy rains it can be a little more problematic as there is no footbridge.

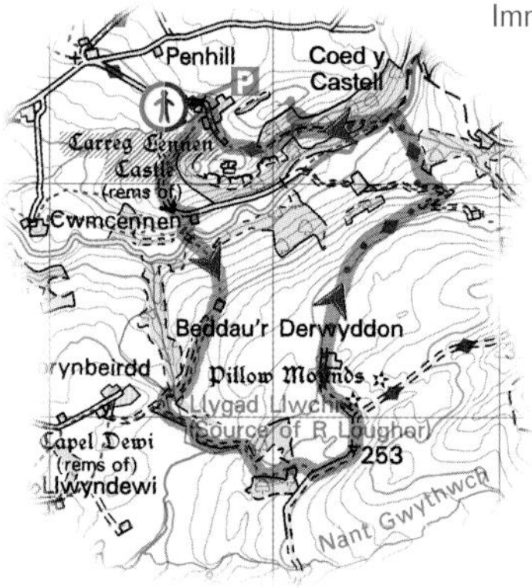

Immediately on the right at this point is a second stile that leads onto a narrow footpath above the river, giving access to a **cave** and the source of the River Loughor. The true source of the river is an underground lake, deep below the Black Mountain, with the infant river emerging here from the Llygad Llwchwr (eye of the Loughor). The cave entrance gives access to a 1200-metre-long system, with a dry high level series, popular with novice speleologists, and a lower active river level that is the preserve of the cave diver. If you wish to visit the entrance, take great care as it can be very slippery.

Cross the stile ahead, proceeding along the track which winds steadily uphill before veering leftward, through a rough pasture, to reach a stile beside a gate and once over, go right to reach a road. Turn left along the road which runs along the lower slopes of the Y Mynydd Du (Black Mountain).

Y Mynydd Du, a rugged and desolate expanse of low nutrition grassland, bogs and rocky outcrops that forms the western section of the Brecon Beacons National Park, is usually referred to by its Welsh

Cattle grazing opposite Carreg Cennen Castle

name in order to distinguish the Carmarthenshire Black Mountain from the Black Mountain in the eastern part of the national park. Tair Carn Uchaf and Tair Carn Isaf, Bronze Age burial mounds, puncture the southern skyline, while Neolithic hut circles, ancient field systems and pillow mounds litter the lower slopes, many now almost invisible among the coarse grasses and rocks.

Walk along the road for 440 metres to where it swings right and here go left along the access drive to Brondai, passing **Beddau'r Derwyddon pillow mounds** on the right, ancient burial mounds thought to date from about 3000BC. ▶ Pass through a gateway leading into the farmyard and here bear left, alongside a fence, to a stile beside another gate giving access onto a rough track which soon gives fine views over Carreg Cennen Castle. At the end of the track turn right, between gates, and along an enclosed grassy footpath to pass through a pedestrian gate, continuing directly ahead through a field

The mounds have doubled as a commercial rabbit warren in more recent times in order to ensure a regular supply of fresh game.

There are impressive views of Carreg Cennen Castle for much of the walk

to a gate and stile. On the far side, follow the footpath alongside a fence to reach a track, bear left along this as it descends into the Cennen Valley once more, and loops sharply round to the left to where the track levels out. Here, climb a stile on the right and follow a pleasant, tree-lined footpath that eventually descends to a footbridge over a stream. Go left on the far side and over a stile to reach a second footbridge spanning the clear waters of the River Cennen once more.

On the far side bear right for a short distance before swinging sharply left and ascending a delightful footpath through the steeply sloping **Coed y Castle** (Wood of the Castle) with numerous benches on which to take a breather or simply enjoy the beauty of this splendid woodland that is both a local Nature Reserve and a designated SSSI.

One of the **underlying geological features** that make this 39-acre Nature Reserve so special is the fact that it has two distinct rock types present that make up the Brecon Beacons. Due to a geological fault that runs through the wood, both limestone and sandstone appear, allowing for two distinct habitats to have developed, with oaks enjoying the Old Red Sandstone soils in the east of the reserve and ash the limestone to the west.

Continue up the slope to eventually reach the entrance gateway to **Carreg Cennen Castle**, the centrepiece during much of this walk and one of the finest fortresses in the whole of Wales, which is well worth exploring. ▶

During the summer months you can buy tickets from the little kiosk at the entrance, but at other times please purchase tickets from the farm.

The position of **Carreg Cennen Castle** is in itself striking, being perched on the edge of a 300ft precipice above the Cennen Valley, with commanding views in all directions giving it spectacular defensive qualities. Possibly built on the site of an earlier Iron Age hill fort, the castle was almost certainly the work of Rhys ap Gruffudd, Prince of the Deheubarth Dynasty of southwest Wales, who built the neighbouring castles at Dryslwyn and Dinefwr, both of which also sit astride the summits of rocky outcrops in the Tywi Valley. The original Welsh castle dates from the late 1100s, but little of that now remains with much of the surviving building being that of an English castle built in the late 13th and early 14th centuries.

Follow the surfaced footpath beneath the northern battlements of the castle and down towards Castle Farm, a centre for rare breed British sheep and cattle, including Longhorn Cattle, Balwen and Soay Sheep. Walk through the farmyard with the gift shop and café on the left and back to the car park.

WALK 17

Carmarthen Fan

Start/Finish	Parking area at the end of the road from Llanddeusant, just beyond Blaenau Farm (SN 796 239)
Distance	14km (8½ miles); shortcut 11km (7 miles); extension 15.5km (9½ miles)
Ascent	685m (2245ft); shortcut 545m (1780ft); extension 700m (2315ft)
Time	4–6hrs; shortcut 3½–5½hrs; extension 4½–6½hrs
Maps	Outdoor Leisure 12
Refreshments	None
Public transport	None

This is an exacting outing that covers some of the most spectacular and remote mountain terrain in the Brecon Beacons National Park. From the parking area at the road head, beyond Llanddeusant, the walk climbs steadily to reach the dark, brooding waters of Llyn y Fan Fach, from where it skirts beneath the steep, shattered cliffs of Picws Du and Fan Foel to reach the narrow spur running down from the latter. A steep climb up to the summit, followed by an optional extension to Fan Brycheiniog, before one of the finest ridge walks in Wales is undertaken, across the peaks of the Carmarthen Fan, with buzzards, ravens, the occasional kite and outstanding scenery for company. The descent is fairly straight forward, but can be a little boggy on the lower slopes of Carnau Llwydion.

From the car park, continue along the surfaced track that climbs steadily towards the valley, with the rushing waters of the **River Sawdde** to the right, but just before reaching the trout farm, roughly halfway to the valley, go left through a gap in the wall and onto a footpath running to the left of the fish hatchery, before rejoining the track. Just before a small building below the lake, the track swings left, passing just left of the dam wall to reach a leet, which acts as a water catchment for the lake.

From here, join a footpath running alongside the leet for 500 metres, and where the leet ends, bear right on a narrow and initially indistinct footpath that runs alongside the **Afon Sychlwch**, climbing steadily towards the steep cliffs that rise menacingly to the rim of the escarpment above. Eventually, a broader, more obvious path is joined and followed leftwards, passing an overhanging, rock outcrop where the path becomes quite narrow for a short distance, then forks just beyond this point. ▶ To continue the main walk, stay on the narrower path that continues to skirt beneath the cliffs, eventually climbing to join the obvious spur running down from Fan Foel.

For a shorter outing, go right and climb the steep zigzags to rejoin the walk just east of the summit of Picws Du at Bwlch Blaen-Twrch.

Turn right at this point, joining a more clearly defined path that climbs steeply up the narrow spur towards the summit of **Fan Foel**, with Llyn y Fan Fawr now visible a short distance to the southeast. Since reaching the spur, the walk has drifted over the county boundary into Powys, but on reaching the top of Fan Foel at 781m (2562ft), it's possible to have one foot in Carmarthenshire and the other in Powys, as the county boundary runs straight through the summit cairn.

Extension to Fan Brycheiniog

For those of you who enjoy 'collecting' summits, it's well worth staying in Powys for the short hop to **Fan Brycheiniog**, just 700 metres to

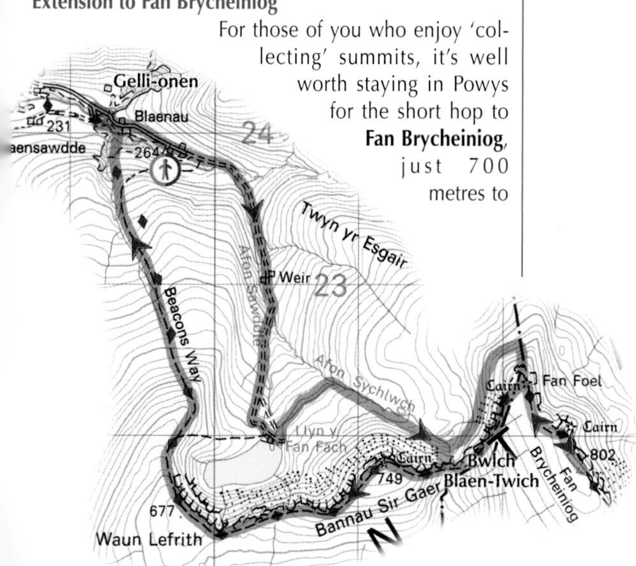

the southeast, with the added bonuses of it being the highest top in the Black Mountains at 802m (2631ft) and with a stone shelter that is a great spot for lunch. There are lovely views down over Llyn y Fan Fawr, with rock shelves projecting from the rim of the steep cliff, out over the void that tumbles dramatically towards the lake below. From Fan Brycheiniog, retrace your steps back to Fan Foel.

At Fan Foel, bear westwards on an obvious footpath along the rim of the escarpment, descending steadily to **Bwlch Blaen-Twrch** with its tiny stream. A fairly steep ascent now follows towards Picws Du (Black Peak), easing slightly as the summit cairn is reached at 749m, with remarkable views down over **Llyn y Fan Fach**, across the Sawdde Valley towards the Glasfynydd Forest that surrounds Usk Reservoir, and extending on into the Cambrian Mountains of Mid Wales. The path now runs along the rim of **Bannau Sir Gaer**, eventually bearing round to the right, high above the western end of the Llyn y Fan Fach, where there are memorable views over the shimmering surface of the lake and back along the line of steep, shattered cliffs of the Carmarthen Fan.

It is quite easy to see why the **isolated waters** of the lake, the appearance of which changes dramatically in different light, has a number of myths and legends associated with it. After all, the Celts attached great importance to water, with lakes and rivers being seen as gateways to the gods and where offerings could be made in order to gain favour and power. The most well known legend associated with Llyn y Fan Fach is 'The Lady of The Lake', the story of which can be read on an information board in the car park at the start of the walk. It is also linked to the 'Physicians of Myddfai'.

The path now begins to descend towards the valley where it soon forks, the right hand branch dropping steeply towards the outflow from the lake to rejoin the

The beautiful Llyn y Fan Fach

outward track, while the left hand branch, and the one the walk follows, continues directly ahead along the edge of a grassy spur. The grassy footpath becomes less distinct as it steadily descends the hillside, following an almost northerly direction and heading for the buildings at **Gelli-onen** on the far side of the valley. On the lower reaches of the grassy hillside, the path can become quite boggy in places before crossing a rough track onto the continuation path alongside a wire fence and descending steeply into a sheep penning area. Pass through a wooden gate, cross a shallow stream and continue along a rough track that bears left above the River Sawdde to a gate giving access onto a farm track. Turn right along the track, crossing the bridge spanning the river to a T-junction with the road and follow this to the right, back to the car park.

WALK 18

Foel Fraith and Garreg Lwyd

Start/Finish	Herbert's Quarry car park on A4069 (SN 730 193)
Distance	14km (8½ miles)
Ascent	515m (1690ft)
Time	4–6hrs
Maps	Outdoor Leisure 12
Refreshments	None
Public transport	None

In predominantly upland moorland on Y Mynydd Du (the Black Mountain), the westernmost section of the Brecon Beacons, this walk follows clear footpaths and old green lanes for the most part, yet it has a very remote feel. The section from the tiny lake at Blaenllynfell, over Foel Fraith, Garreg Lwyd, Foel Fawr and back down to the A4069 is less distinct and could cause difficulty in low cloud and mist. In fact, it would be somewhat wasteful, as well as being more navigationally difficult, to attempt this walk in anything but good weather, as the views from the high summits over the Brecon Beacons and into Mid Wales are nothing short of spectacular. The walk also passes sites of historic and prehistoric interest, with industrial archaeological dominating to an extent.

Quarry spoil litters the landscape here: a mixture of small and large excavations, old lime kilns and access tracks, the remains of what was once a rich and extensive industry that provided considerable employment for the local area. Limestone and silica sand has been quarried in this area since 1730, with the quarries on Foel Fawr last being worked in the 1930s. The job was probably pretty tough at the best of times, but working outside, on the quarry faces, during the winter months must have been particularly harsh, as this area catches the full force of the weather. The quarried limestone was burnt in the kilns to form quicklime, much of which was used to 'sweeten' fields and make them less acidic, but also for making mortar in the building industry. Silica sand was used as an industrial cleaner, being highly abrasive and similar in structure to particles of Millstone Grit.

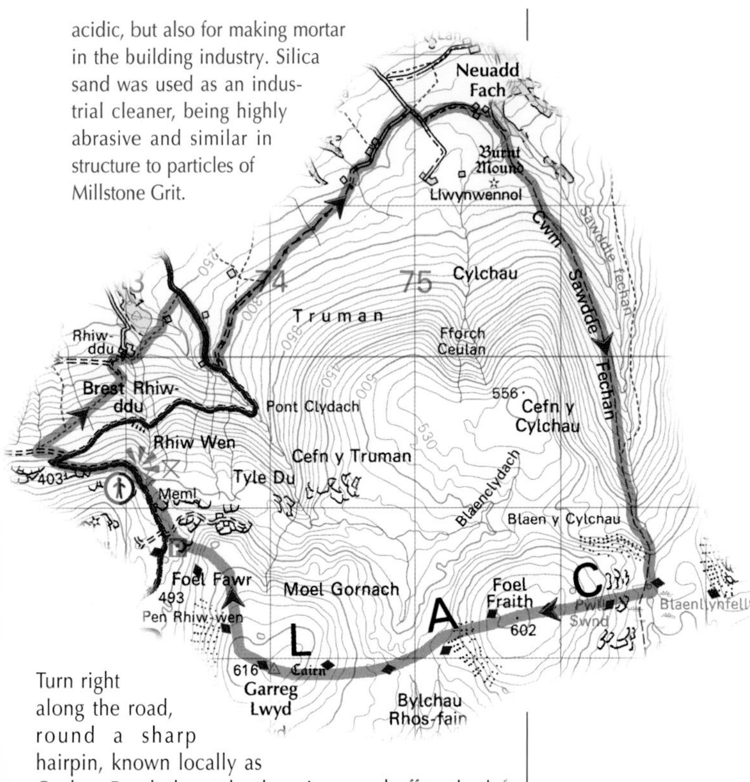

Turn right along the road, round a sharp hairpin, known locally as Cuckoo Bend, then take the minor road off to the left towards Trapp. After 200 metres, turn sharp right onto a faint track, running parallel to the main road initially, which soon becomes more distinct as it descends the hillside, eventually swinging round to the left to a junction with another track, alongside a waymarker post, and here go right. Where the track swings left, towards buildings at **Rhiw-ddu**, turn right, off the track, passing to the right of a barn on a narrow track that crosses two small streams before swinging right towards the property at Pant-y-bedw. When almost opposite the property, go left off the track and descend to cross a footbridge spanning the

Approaching the ford below Neuadd Fach

Afon Clydach, bear left on the opposite side and through iron gates beside a barn. Walk past the barn, cross the entrance to the farmyard onto a zigzag path that climbs up a bank, crosses a stile leading onto the access drive and turn left to the road.

Follow the road rightwards, cross a cattle grid, then 100 metres beyond this, turn sharp left onto a broad track that skirts the foot of the Black Mountain, with superb views to the left into the Cambrian Mountains and Mid Wales. Eventually the track reaches buildings at Ty-newydd, where the walk continues along the surfaced access lane to a T-junction with a minor road. Turn right along the lane for 80 metres, then go left, through a gate, onto a track along the left edge of fields and towards buildings at **Neuadd Fach**. Pass through the gate giving access to the farmyard, following an enclosed track to the right of the farm, that leads down to a ford over the Afon Ceulan, and once over bear right to start the ascent up the **Cwm Sawdde Fechan**.

The track up the side of the valley is stony at first, but soon becomes grass covered as it passes through a gate in a stock fence to enter Open Access Land. As it climbs it becomes less distinct, eventually passing to the right of an old sheepfold on the side of the stream, from where it virtually disappears. From here it's a case of picking the driest, most pleasant way possible up the head of the valley, but always keeping on the right side of the stream to where the valley narrows and the path becomes a little more defined. As the path crosses the watershed between Cwm Sawdde Fechan to the north and the Afon Twrch to the south, now with amazing views southwards, a small mountain pool, named **Blaenflynfell**, is passed on the left. Some 100 metres beyond the pool, bear right and start the climb up the eastern slopes of Foel Fraith, walking through tussocky grass with no obvious footpath, but following a range of sheep tracks.

The route passes **pot holes and shake holes**, places where the limestone below has been eroded by underground streams, causing the rock above to collapse, forming small hollows, or, in some cases, large depressions in the grass.

Despite the lack of a distinct footpath, the ascent is fairly easy and the exposed, rounded summit of **Foel Fraith** is soon reached. ▶ Continue over the summit, following a course slightly south of due west, until the ground begins to slope away on its western side and here veer slightly leftwards, on a very indistinct footpath that descends into a shallow valley. From here, the more obvious footpath up to the summit of **Garreg Lwyd** is clearly visible, on the opposite side of the valley, so pick the easiest, driest route across the valley floor to join the footpath and follow it onto the summit, the high point of the walk at 616m (2021ft), with more far reaching views.

This is a good place to stop and drink in the magnificent views, which are some of the finest in Carmarthenshire.

On the **summit** of Garreg Lwyd, there is both a cairn and a separate OS trig point, a somewhat unusual occurrence. The cairn is huge and constructed on the true summit, while the trig point, unusual in itself in that it is of stone construction and not poured concrete, is set slightly off to the

A waterfall high in the Cwm Sawdde Fechan

side. This is in respect of the ancient summit cairn, a practice that has, sadly, not always been followed, the trig points being built right on top of the cairn in what can only be described as an act of official vandalism.

From the summit cairn, follow a faint footpath in a northwesterly direction, heading towards a large, isolated boulder some 400 metres away, but after 200 metres, bear right and begin to descend, now in a northerly direction down the broad, grassy ridge of **Foel Fawr**. The indistinct path eventually veers leftwards, passing a stone cairn and heading for a car park on the side of the A4069, but 100 metres before reaching the road, bear right on a narrow path that runs past old spoil heaps and quarries. Cross a broad track heading into quarry workings on the right, continuing past the largest of the ruined lime kilns and a **memorial plaque** to David Davies, with Herbert's Quarry car park just beyond.

Burry Port Marina (Walks 20 and 22)

WALK 19

Loughor Bridge to Llanelli North Dock

Start	Loughor Bridge (SS 560 981)
Finish	Llanelli North Dock (SS 497 994)
Distance	10.5km (6½ miles)
Ascent	40m (125ft)
Time	3–4hrs
Maps	Explorer 164
Refreshments	Several pubs and cafés along the way
Public transport	Bus 110/111 Swansea–Carmarthen stops near the beginning and end of the walk. Frequent service, 7 days a week.

Loughor Bridge, as its name suggests, spans the River Loughor, which forms the county boundary in this part of Carmarthenshire. This is a very straightforward section of the Wales Coast Path, being well waymarked, with negligible ascent and on good surfaces throughout. There are superb views over the estuary to the rolling, fertile hills of north Gower and depending on the time of year and state of the tide, you may see flocks of waders feeding on the mudflats. If you would like to guarantee a peek at some of the area's wildlife, pop into the National Wetlands area, a 450-acre nature reserve part way along the route.

From the Carmarthenshire County Boundary sign, on the west side of **Loughor Bridge**, descend a flight of steps on the north side of the busy A484 onto a lane, follow this to its end and go left along Yspitty Road, passing the Schaeffer UK bearings factory and the Lewis Arms pub on the right. At a junction with the B4297, cross to Bynea Gate car park on the opposite side, walk round its left hand side, passing a notice board proclaiming the start of the **Millennium Coastal Park**, then turn left along a surfaced footpath which is followed, with a turn first right, then left, to a footbridge spanning the railway line and A484.

In a little over 10 years, the **22.5km ofcoastline** from Bynea Gate westward to Pwll has been

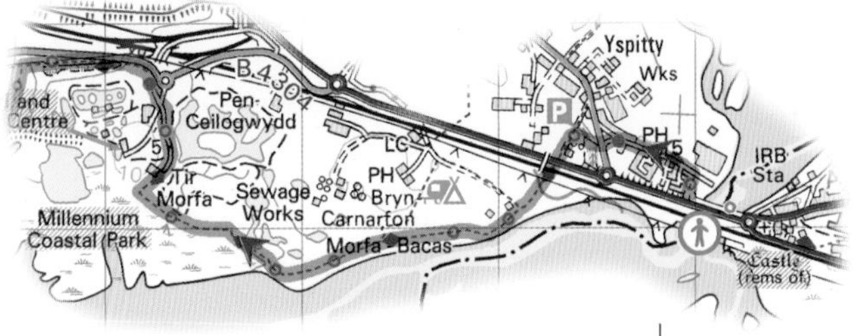

map continues on page 122

transformed from 1000ha of industrial abuse and dereliction into a green oasis of tourist attractions, wildlife habitats and leisure facilities known as the Millennium Coastal Park. The park, as the name suggests, was created to celebrate the turn of the new millennium and was funded, among others, by the National Lottery, Carmarthenshire County Council, the Welsh Assembly and the EU. The project was huge, but the results are something to behold, with

The Loughor Estuary

thousands flocking to the area for recreation and relaxation, rather than for a 12-hour shift in some of the dirtiest and most environmentally hazardous workplaces in the UK.

From here, the continuation footpath is obvious as it skirts the north side of the Loughor Estuary, also known as the Burry Inlet, with fabulous views all the way along the northern side of the Gower.

The estuary here is within the **Carmarthen Bay Special Area of Conservation** and is an SSSI. Look out for flocks of dunlin, ringed plover, sanderling and redshank along the shoreline, with curlew, oystercatcher and shelduck further out on the mudflats.

Eventually the path turns inland in order to pass through the **National Wetlands Centre Wales**, on the Bury Inlet, where it is possible to see wild birds up to 50,000 strong during the winter months. ◂

The café is open to the public even if you don't wish to visit, although this is highly recommended.

Cross the access road to the reserve then go left on a track that runs parallel with the road before swinging back towards the coast alongside the award-winning **Machynys Peninsula golf course**.

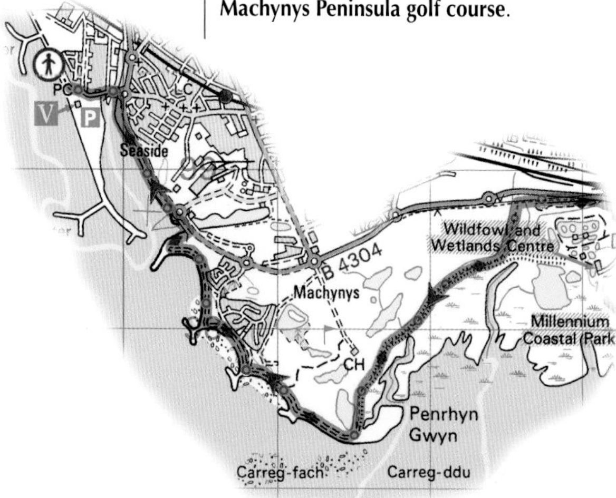

Modern apartment blocks at North Dock

The **golf course**, designed by Jack Nicklaus, opened in 2005 after a staggering build cost in excess of £3.5 million. It consists of a necklace of ponds and lakes, wetland areas and ditch systems that are designed to attract wildlife to the area. The rare and threatened water vole can be found here along with ever increasing numbers of otters.

The route continues round Machynys Bay and past a new development of attractive properties, then swings inland alongside a tidal inlet towards a road. Before reaching the road, go left over the bridge spanning the inlet and follow the cycleway/footpath as it runs alongside the road. At the second roundabout, veer left over footbridges at **North Dock**, where you will find the Discovery Centre, along with an information centre and a very pleasant first floor café with a balcony seating area giving splendid views over the bay and along the coast.

WALK 20

Llanelli North Dock to Burry Port Harbour

Start	Llanelli North Dock (SS 497 994)
Finish	Burry Port Harbour (SN 444 004)
Distance	7km (4½ miles)
Ascent	40m (130ft)
Time	2–2½hrs
Maps	Explorer 164
Refreshments	Several pubs and cafés along the way
Public transport	Bus 110/111 Swansea–Carmarthen stops near the beginning and end of the walk. Frequent service, 7 days a week. Trains also run back to Llanelli from Burry Harbour.

This very easy but enjoyable section of the Wales Coast Path makes an excellent wet weather alternative when footpaths inland tend to be boggy, being on well surfaced footpaths throughout. It can also be combined with Walk 19 and Walk 22. Llanelli North Dock, once a busy area that echoed to the sound of cargo ships being loaded with the products of Llanelli's various industries, is now a very pleasant 'marina' with a Discovery Centre that also acts as a tourist information centre and refreshment stop. Much of the walk passes through the Millennium Coastal Park, an area created from the land where tinworks, brickworks and various other industries once stood, before arriving at the very pleasant harbour area of Burry Port.

North Dock Dunes Local Nature Reserve, found just to the south of the Discovery Centre, is worth a visit before starting out on the walk. It is home to many specialist plants and animals. The rare Marbled White butterfly inhabits these dunes, along with Sea Holly and Sea Campion to name but a few, all of which are specially adapted to withstand this dry, sandy habitat.

From the Discovery Centre, bear right along the coastal footpath, on a broad, surfaced track with numerous benches, picnic areas and viewing platforms, to climb over a small hill through which runs the railway. The hill sports a tapering steel tower, one of several along the way that symbolises the Millennium Coastal Park. On the far side is **Sandy Water Park**, an area which consists of a 16-acre lake with flocks of resident ducks and swans. Just beyond this is Festival Fields, built for the 2000 National Eisteddfod, followed shortly by the Pavilion Café on the right.

Just beyond the café is a small, inauspicious memorial to Amelia Earhart.

Following Charles Lindbergh's **solo flight across the Atlantic** in 1927, there was considerable interest as to who would be the first female to undertake such a dangerous crossing. Although Amelia Earhart

map continues on page 126

One of many benches along the Wales Coast Path near North Dock, Llanelli

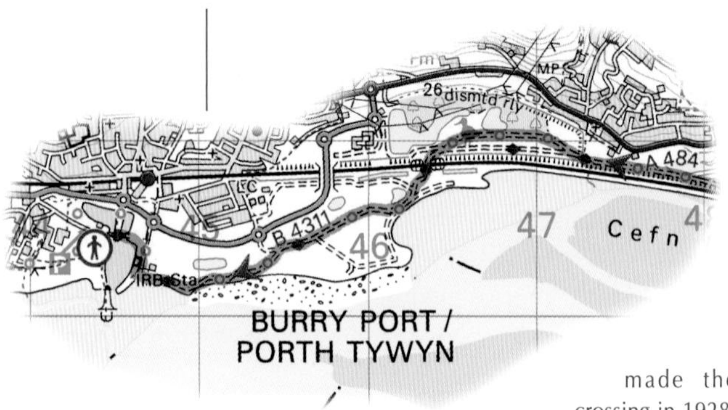

made the crossing in 1928, flying from Trepassey Harbour, Newfoundland on the 17 June and landing in the estuary near here on the 18, it was not a solo flight, the aircraft being piloted by Wilmer Stultz, with Earhart as a passenger.

It's possible to continue directly ahead, on a rough track, that runs parallel with the railway line before rejoining the main path just before a bridge spanning the line.

A little further along, the surfaced Wales Coast Path (WCP) veers to the right. ◀ Just beyond the bridge the WCP swings rightwards and passes to the right of a small hill where wind generators once stood. On reaching a small car park, take the second exit on the left, signed to Burry Port and continue westward with more superb views over the bay to eventually reach **Burry Port Harbour**, the newest marina in Wales with a capacity to berth 450 boats. Follow the footpath around the marina, passing the lifeboat building and crossing two footbridges to reach a car park on the far side.

WALK 21

Cwm Lliedi Reservoir and Parc Howard

Start/Finish	Parking area at northern end of Cwm Lliedi Reservoir (SN 515 042)
Distance	9km (5½ miles)
Ascent	210m (690ft)
Time	3hrs
Maps	Explorer 178
Refreshments	Soft drinks and ice cream at Parc Howard; all options in Llanelli
Public transport	Bus 128 Llanelli–Ammanford (services Mon-Sat) runs along the A476, passing close to the southern end of the reservoir.

The upper and lower Lliedi reservoirs nestle in the picturesque Swiss Valley, just north of Llanelli. Because of their proximity to a large urban population, they have become an important amenity site for the area, with cycle routes, wheelchair friendly surfaces, well marked trails and walks, fishing points for anglers on the upper reservoir, launch points for canoeists on the lower reservoir and both being a haven for wildlife. This is a very pleasant walk that dips into both rural and urban parts of the region by following a dismantled railway line along Swiss Valley to Parc Howard. Due to the generally excellent underfoot surfaces along the length of this walk, it is a good option for the times of year when fields and hills are wet and muddy.

From the small car park, join the footpath that runs around the eastern end of the reservoir, initially crossing a small footbridge over a boggy area before ascending through woodland and walking alongside a metal tubular rail that guards a drop down a steep bank. The path soon descends to lower levels, with tantalising glimpses of the water through the trees that fringe the banks of **Cwm Lliedi Reservoir**.

The **reservoirs** were constructed to provide a reliable and clean source of water for the growing metal

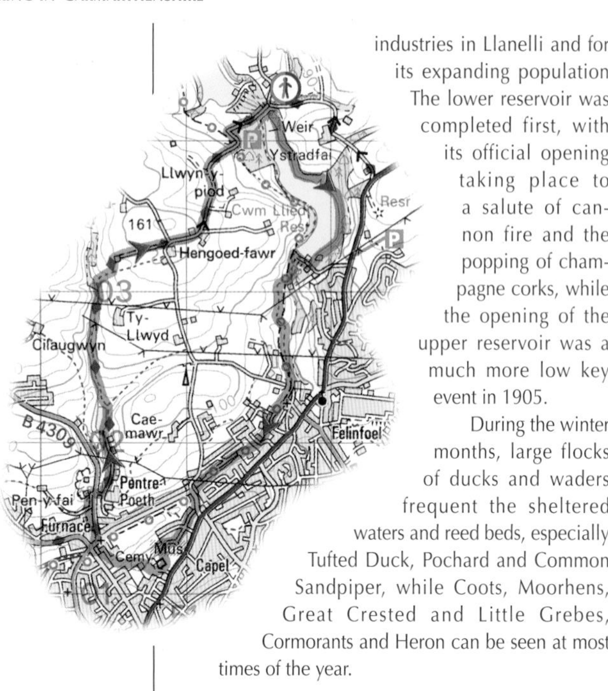

industries in Llanelli and for its expanding population The lower reservoir was completed first, with its official opening taking place to a salute of cannon fire and the popping of champagne corks, while the opening of the upper reservoir was a much more low key event in 1905.

During the winter months, large flocks of ducks and waders frequent the sheltered waters and reed beds, especially Tufted Duck, Pochard and Common Sandpiper, while Coots, Moorhens, Great Crested and Little Grebes, Cormorants and Heron can be seen at most times of the year.

At the end of the reservoir bear right along the retaining wall, now with good views to the right along its length, then veer left on the far side on a footpath that enters woodland high above the Afon Lliedi which can be heard rushing through the valley below.

At a fork in the path keep right and after a brief ascent bear left along the old railway line that now serves as a surfaced footpath and part of the Swiss Valley Cycleway.

The **Swiss Valley Cycleway** runs from the Millennium Coastal Park at Llanelli to Mynydd Mawr Woodland Park at Tumble. It forms one arm of the Celtic Cycle Trail network, which provides over 320km of off-road coastal and countryside cycling.

Cormorants ignore the 'scare' streamers on Cwm Lliedi Reservoir

The old line provides very pleasant and easy walking, initially through countryside with views across Swiss Valley to the left, then past houses on the edge of **Felinfoel**, one of the northern suburbs of Llanelli. Immediately before the first bridge spanning the old line, go right and climb up to the road which is taken to the left, initially crossing over the dismantled line, for 150 metres, where a short surfaced footpath on the right gives access to Parc Howard Avenue. At the 'T' junction at the far end of the road go right, still in Parc Howard Avenue, following this round to the left and through an iron gate that gives access to the grounds of Parc Howard. Once through, go left up a flight of steps, following the surfaced footpath through the lawns to reach **Parc Howard Museum** on the right.

Follow the surfaced footpath round to the right and alongside the fence of the well manicured bowling green, and then descend a flight of steps at the end, but before doing so, look to the left for fine views over the River Loughor estuary and into Gower. At the bottom of the

PARC HOWARD MANSION

Parc Howard Mansion is a country house, once known as Bryncaerau Park and originally the home of Mr R T Howell, a well known businessman and Harbour Commissioner. When he died, the house passed to James Buckley Wilson who transformed the building into the Italianate mansion of today. The house and grounds were sold in 1911 to Sir Stafford Howard who purchased them in order to be able to gift them to the people of Llanelli but with a proviso. In January 1912, Sir Stafford and Lady Howard Stepney presented the mansion to the town, granting the Council a 999-year lease, but insisting that they transform the gardens and grounds into a public amenity within eight months. There were two reasons for this condition; one being that he wished the gardens to be open on the first anniversary of his wedding to Lady Howard. The second was his belief that the local authorities were a little slow at performing their duties and this was a way of enforcing progress. The mansion now houses a museum that is best known for its large collection of Llanelli Pottery, along with paintings, portraits and other art works and artefacts relating to the local area. It opens Tuesday–Friday 10am–1pm, 2–5pm, and Saturday 1–5pm.

steps bear left for 40 metres then right along a sloping footpath with the park's paddling pool down to the left. Keep left of the children's adventure playground and join a narrow surfaced footpath that descends into trees and exits from the park and a junction with Lakeview Terrace. Go right along this, crossing the dismantled railway line and turning left at the end of the road to a junction with Ynys y Cwm Road in **Furnace**. Follow this to the right, passing the Stradley Hotel on the right, then go right after 300 metres along the access drive to **Craig Wen**, which quickly bears left along a track and passes to the left of said property, before a junction with another track in front of the retaining bank of a large, attractive lily pond. Bear right along the track, keeping directly ahead alongside a timber fence where this swings left through a gate, joining a narrower footpath through trees, with a small stream for company to the left.

This section of footpath and the rest of the walk back to the start is part of St Illtyd's Walk, a 103km long-distance walk that stretches from Pembrey Country Park in the west to Mergam Park, Port Talbot, in the east.

◀ The footpath heads out into countryside once more, passing through a series of kissing gates as it does

so, before eventually being forced to the right, where it makes a series of steep zig-zags between gorse and bramble thickets. It soon becomes a grassy, fence enclosed footpath between fields with lovely views in all directions before skirting to the left of **Cwtta Farm** and joining its access drive. Follow this out to the road and go left, then almost immediately right on a narrow lane that descends back to the car park at **Cwm Lliedi**.

Parc Howard Mansion is now a museum

WALK 22

Burry Port Harbour to Kidwelly

Start	Burry Port Harbour (SN 444 004)
Finish	Station Road car park, Kidwelly (SN 406 670)
Distance	17km (10½ miles)
Ascent	70m (230ft)
Time	4–6hrs
Maps	Explorer 164
Refreshments	Several pubs and cafés along the way
Public transport	Bus 110/111 Swansea–Carmarthen stops near the beginning and end of the walk. Frequent service, 7 days a week. For Kidwelly, bus 198/199 runs the route Carmarthen–Kidwelly–Llanelli.

Situated in the middle of the Millennium Coastal Park, Burry Port is a very attractive harbour and Wales' newest marina. Although the initial part of this section of the Wales Coastal Footpath runs along Pembrey Burrows, with fine, open views across Carmarthen Bay to the Gower, much of it follows an inland route, passing through Pembrey Forest, an artificial forest planted in the 1930s. It then follows surfaced tracks and roads through fields before a short roadside section leads to a very interesting part of the walk along Kymers Canal before reaching Kidwelly.

map continues on page 134

From the car park on the west side of Burry Port Harbour, walk towards the **pier**, with the lighthouse, built in 1842, at the far end, but just before reaching the buildings of the sailing club, bear right along a surfaced track past houses and across waste ground to a

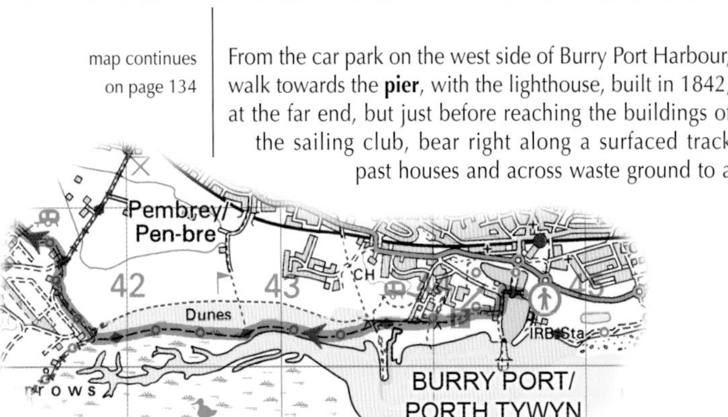

Kite buggies on Pembrey Sands

T-junction with another track. Turn left along this, passing impressive sand dunes on the left and a caravan park on the right. Cross a small parking area near **Pembrey Harbour**, continuing along the Wales Coast Path (WCP), with several seating areas along this stretch of the route offering fine views over Pembrey Sands and Carmarthen Bay.

Eventually you reach Pembrey Gateway, an area of large stone pillars with timber additions, marking the entrance to **Pembrey Forest Country Park**. At this point the WCP goes right, away from the coast, and follows a surfaced track that runs past a parking area to a road that gives vehicle access to the Country Park. Cross the road and join a broad, stony track on the far side, go through a gateway and head into the forest, passing a **caravan park** on the left. Several paths and trails run off into the forest on both sides of the main track, allowing visitors to explore the deeper recesses of the park.

At a fork in the track, approximately 2km after entering the forest, keep straight ahead (waymarker) on a slightly less defined track. You may come across areas where the track is a little churned up or strewn with bark and lined with logs. This is because Pembrey is an actively managed forest, where felling and replanting activities take place throughout the year. At a junction with a surfaced track, turn right and follow this for 800 metres to reach a waymarker pointing leftwards onto an old concrete military road that runs between fields on the edge of Pembrey airfield. Pass through a gateway and turn immediately right along another concrete track, eventually swinging slightly leftward with buildings in Kidwelly now visible directly ahead. At a junction with a much broader track, close to old military buildings, continue directly ahead for 20 metres, then turn left round the base of an old building, through a gate and up a flight of steps to a surfaced footpath running along the top of a flood defence on the edge of the salt marsh.

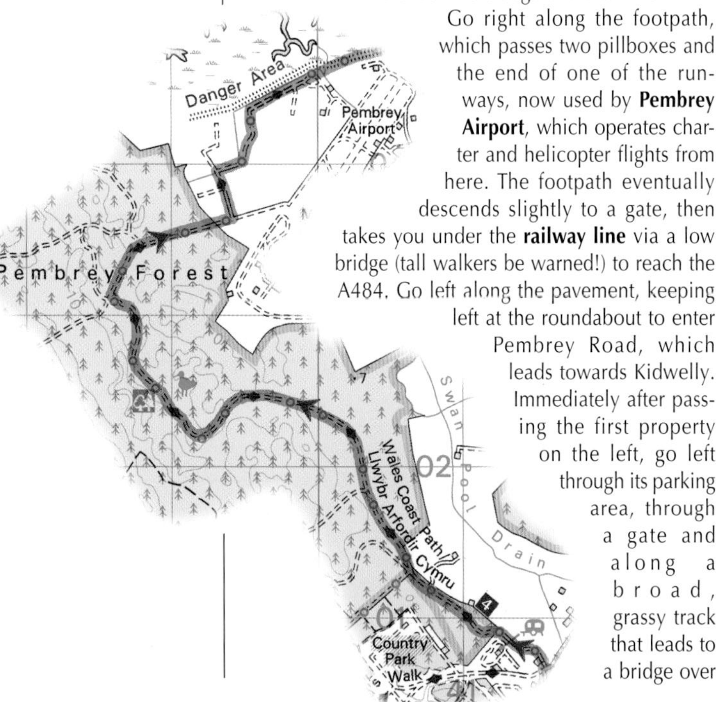

Go right along the footpath, which passes two pillboxes and the end of one of the runways, now used by **Pembrey Airport**, which operates charter and helicopter flights from here. The footpath eventually descends slightly to a gate, then takes you under the **railway line** via a low bridge (tall walkers be warned!) to reach the A484. Go left along the pavement, keeping left at the roundabout to enter Pembrey Road, which leads towards Kidwelly. Immediately after passing the first property on the left, go left through its parking area, through a gate and along a broad, grassy track that leads to a bridge over the railway line. Once over, go through a kissing gate and turn right to walk round the edge of a field to reach another gate leading to Kymer's Canal. Turn left and walk along whichever side of this you choose, as both options lead to **Kidwelly Quay** picnic area and car park overlooking the Afon Gwendraeth estuary.

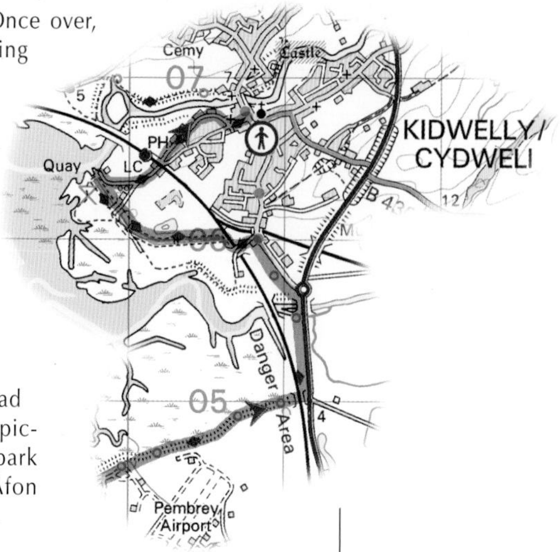

The **river estuary** has played an important part in the history and industrial development of Kidwelly. In medieval times, the castle could receive supplies from the sea, as the Gwendraeth Fach was navigable into Kidwelly town. However, shifting sands in the estuary made passage difficult at times and hampered the development of the area, so in order to improve access the quay was built here by Thomas Kymer. It opened in 1768, as did Kymer's Canal, the earliest industrial canal to be built in Wales, which linked his coal pits along the Gwendraeth Fawr with the quay. The quay remained in use through to the early 1920s, when it was abandoned and became derelict. It was finally restored in the 1980s and later given listed building status in recognition of its importance to Welsh industrial history. The quay is a superb place to observe waders on the river, especially during the winter months when great flocks of birds can be seen feeding on the mudflats.

A train crosses the Afon Gwendraeth at Kidwelly

From Kidwelly Quay, walk through the car park and along the access road towards **Kidwelly**, crossing the railway line and the turning for Kidwelly Station on the edge of town. For those wishing to return to Burry Port by train, terminate your walk at this point. To continue, walk on past Anthony's Hotel and along Hillfield Villas to a T-junction at its end and go left into Station Road, to reach Bridge Street, opposite St Mary's Church.

WALK 23

Kidwelly and the Gwendraeth Valley

Start/Finish	Station Road car park, Kidwelly (SN 406 670)
Distance	13km (8 miles)
Ascent	295m (970ft)
Time	4–5hrs
Maps	Explorer 177
Refreshments	All kinds in Kidwelly
Public transport	Trains from Swansea, Llanelli and Carmarthen on the main Cardiff–Fishguard line. Also buses 110/111 Swansea–Llanelli–Kidwelly and 198/199 Carmarthen–Kidwelly–Llanelli.

Kidwelly and its quieter surroundings are fascinating places to explore, with a huge range of geographical locations that vary from coastal salt marsh through to almost mountain habitat. As one would expect with such a variance in environments, the wildlife that one may see is also extremely diverse, with flocks of wading birds and salt loving plants on the marshes, through to many birds of prey and upland and woodland plant species on Mynydd y Garreg Mountain. The walk initially passes through Kidwelly then out to Kymers Quay and the Carmarthen Bay salt marshes before heading back inland for an ascent of Mynydd y Garreg. It then crosses the Gwendraeth Valley before returning to Kidwelly via the lovely Summer Way.

Turn right out of the car park and walk to the very end of Station Road, going left into Quay Road and over the railway line. ▸ Where the road forks keep right and follow this to **Kidwelly Quay**. (See Walk 22 for information on the quay.)

If you arrive by train, start the walk from here.

Cross the canal at the far end of the car park and follow the surfaced footpath round the edge of the picnic area and salt marsh, bearing right after 200 metres over a footbridge and continuing to eventually reach a bridge spanning Kymer's Canal. Turn right along the side of the canal and at its end go right through a pedestrian gate to join a footpath round the edge of a field and alongside the **railway line**. Cross a bridge over the railway line and follow a broad grassy track past a B&B to reach the road on the outskirts of Kidwelly.

Turn left along the roadside footpath for 200 metres, then cross onto the access drive for Beynon Davies Concrete Products, bearing left almost immediately onto a bridleway that follows a dismantled railway line along the southern side of Kidwelly. At a junction with a partly surfaced lane bear right, cross the A484, then join the drive to Dyfrig Dalziel Ltd, but turn right after a few metres to pass through a gate then go almost immediately left through a second gate (public bridleway sign on the fence) to rejoin the dismantled railway line. At a junction with a lane keep right, passing to the left of houses and at a junction with another lane, cross to a pedestrian gate, continuing along the bridleway to reach yet another lane. Turn left for a few metres before rejoining the bridleway on the right, alongside a bungalow, and walk onto reach the road on the outskirts of **Mynydd y Garreg**. Cross the

A sign near the Old Forge

road and bear right, up through the village, which is also known as 'Stone Mountain'.

At the top of the village, go left along Heol yr Ysgol and follow this for 150 metres, before bearing right in between the school and village hall. Turn right again in 30 metres on a footpath that skirts the school playground, to reach a 'T' junction with a track and go left along this, climbing past old quarry workings on Mynydd y Garreg.

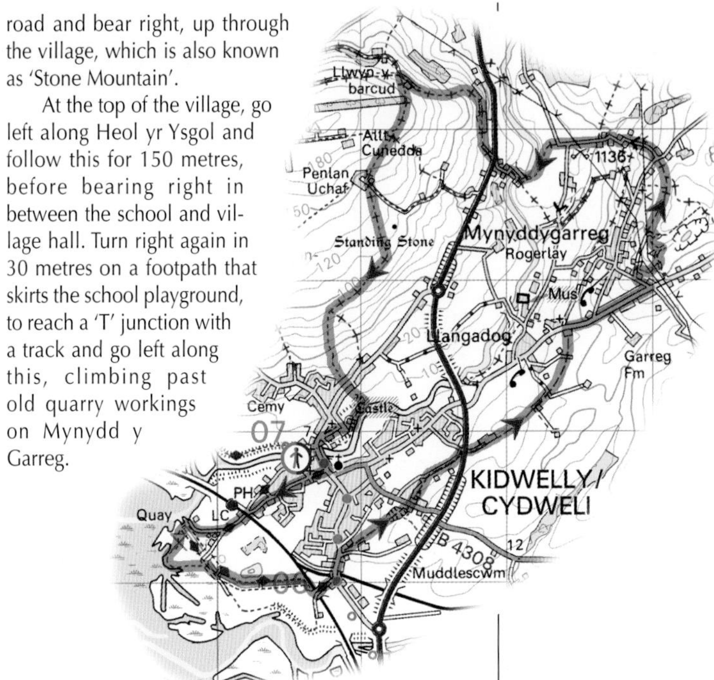

The **quarry** to the right was created during the 19th century when silica was extracted. This did not go down well with the people in the village who put up quite a lot of resistance to the mining company. The standoff became so heated at times that the local papers began calling them the 'Silica Wars'. Today, the quarries are filled with water and, like the rest of the mountain, are a thriving wildlife habitat.

At a junction with a stony track, go left, bearing right after 50 metres onto a broader track and veering left at a Y-fork in a further 75 metres. On reaching Horeb Road, turn left for 40 metres before turning right past cottages

Kidwelly Castle dominates the town

and following a quiet lane that descends the western slopes of 'Stone Mountain', with fine views ahead over the Gwendraeth Fach Valley. Follow the lane for just over 800 metres to where it bends to the right (150 metres after passing beneath power lines) and here climb a stile, directly ahead, into a field which is crossed to its diagonally opposite left hand corner. Negotiate a stile, pass through a section of woodland just above the river and descend onto the access drive to the Old Forge Farm. Turn right along the track, crossing the river and climb up to towards houses where a footpath sign directs you to 'The Rest of the World'!

At a junction with the busy A484, turn left for 30 metres, then bear right up an enclosed track, climbing a stile on the right alongside the second iron field gate into a sloping field and walk up its left hand side before skirting the left edge of King's Wood. Climb a stile, continue round the top of a sloping field to reach a gap through the field fence (waymarker), then walk through the centre of the next field to a gate and on in the same direction through another field. After passing through another gate, bear diagonally left towards the right hand end of farm buildings and a stile leading onto the farm drive, which is followed to the right and a junction of tracks and footpaths. Turn left up a broad, tree-lined track and follow this, with fine views to the left through the trees, to reach a gate leading to **Penlan Uchaf Farm**. Walk through the farmyard, following the red waymarkers, before turning left down the access drive for 150 metres to a gate on the right leading onto a track. ▶

This is a footpath change from that shown on the current map.

At a junction of tracks, go through a gate, climb the stile opposite then follow the permissive waymarkers over a small stream and into a field. Pass between a row of isolated oak trees to a pedestrian gate and follow the very pleasant 'Summer Way'. Where the track bears left, signposted 'Summer Way', climb a stile directly ahead, then bear diagonally left through a field and over a second stile with superb views ahead over Kidwelly, the castle and coast. Bear diagonally right through two fields, passing through hedge gaps, then turn left down the side

Kidwelly from 'The Summer Way'

of a third, sloping field to a stile at the bottom that leads onto an enclosed footpath alongside houses in **Kidwelly**. Cross straight over the road into the lane opposite and once past the children's playground, go left through a pedestrian gate onto a footpath that runs alongside the river and beneath the castle walls. Climb up to the castle car park and the ruins of Kidwelly's spectacular **castle**.

The town is dominated by this very **impressive castle**, which is one of the finest still standing, following the Anglo-Norman subjugation of Wales. The first castle to stand here would have been the earth and timber structure, built by Roger of Salisbury about 1106. Although much of the ruins that we see today are largely from the late 13th and early 14th centuries, with some late medieval and Tudor additions, the current shape was heavily influenced by the original castle. Kidwelly shows some of the more advanced features of castle design from the time, with an inner circuit of defensive walls being built within an outer circuit, allowing the castle to be held even if the outer wall should fall. Also, like several of the castles in southwest Wales, Kidwelly was situated in a coastal area with river access, protecting important coastal shipping routes, but also allowing supplies to reach the castle should the Welsh cut off landward supply routes. A visit is highly recommended.

Bear left along Castle Street and through the old south gate, built around 1300, in Kidwelly's town walls, before turning left along New Street and over the **river** into Bridge Street. Take the first turn on the right back into Station Road.

Amroth Beach (Walk 28)

WALK 24

Llansteffan Castle

Start/Finish	Beach car park, Llansteffan (SN 353 105)
Distance	4km (2½ miles)
Ascent	150m (490ft)
Time	1½hrs
Maps	Explorer 177
Refreshments	Cafés and pubs in Llansteffan
Public transport	Bus 227 Carmarthen–Llan-y-bri. Infrequent services, none Sun.

Very short, but most enjoyable, this walk has one long, steep climb onto the hills above Llansteffan, from where there are superb views over the surrounding countryside. Nestling on the side of the Tywi Estuary, Llansteffan is a lovely little place with a low key seaside atmosphere but with a big history, as can be gauged by its fine castle, which by even Welsh standards, is a spectacular ruin, perched on a craggy hill overlooking the town, estuary and bay beyond. This walk can be combined with Walk 25.

From the surfaced car park at the castle end of the village, follow the enclosed footpath, just to the left of the Beach Café, to a junction with a surfaced lane and turn left. There are fine views across the estuary towards Ferryside to the left, the castle ahead and **Plas Mansion** to the right.

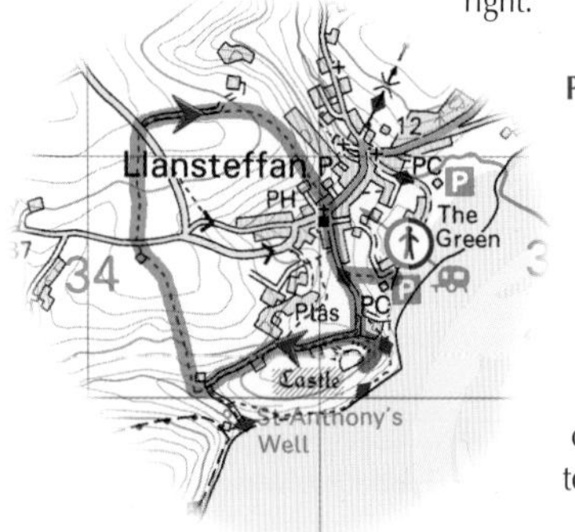

Plas Mansion is a rather grand affair, built in 1788 on the site of a much earlier house of 16th-century construction. The current mansion is built in classical style, with a lovely two-storied facade and a pillared 'Tuscan' portico.

Where the lane forks, keep right, climbing gently to reach a sharp turning off to the left that leads up to **Llansteffan Castle**.

LLANSTEFFAN CASTLE

In a land full of castles, Llansteffan may not be the jewel in the crown, but it is still a mighty impressive structure in a most picturesque location, standing as it does on top of a well-defined headland overlooking the vast expanses of the Tywi Estuary. As one would expect on a site with such defensive and communication potential, the position was first fortified during the Iron Age when a double bank and ditch was excavated across the headland, creating a defensive promontory fort.

Although it's difficult to pin point when the present castle was initially built, it was probably raised by the Normans during their initial invasion of southwest Wales, soon after 1100 when the initial Iron Age ditches were re-cut and a structure known as a 'ringwork' castle, consisting of an earth bank crowned by a timber palisade, was constructed within.

However, it is not until 1146 that the first definite reference to Llansteffan occurs and from then through to the 1260s the castle had a chequered history, changing hands between Welsh and Anglo-Norman occupation several times. The initial stone work would have begun during these conflicts, but it was during the late 13th century that the bulk of what stands here today was erected with other additions during the late 15th century, after which the military importance of the site declined and Llansteffan passed into relative obscurity.

Proceed along the lane, swinging left round a bend and descending to a junction of tracks and paths. Pass

Llansteffan Beach

View over Llansteffan on the return leg

through a gate directly ahead onto the drive to a private house and, at the end of the drive, go through another gate leading into a sloping field. Turn right, climbing alongside the hedge to a stile at the top, then bear left along the left hand side of two more fields to a junction with a lane. Cross this to a stile opposite, walk along the left edge of another field to a gate in the far corner, then head straight across the next field to a stile in the far hedge leading onto another lane. ◂

It's worth stopping occasionally and turning round to enjoy the superb views that are now unfolding.

Bear left across the lane to a track on the opposite side, but where this forks near buildings at Lanfach, veer right off the track and walk alongside a hedge to reach a kissing gate. Once through, continue alongside the right hand hedge of the next three fields, descending to a stile and a footpath enclosed between a high wall on the left and a hedge bank on the right, which leads down to The Square in **Llansteffan**. Cross over the road, passing to the left of the circular Old Pound, a place where stray animals were kept in bygone days, and Llansteffan Church to reach the outward footpath and follow this back to the start.

WALK 25

Llansteffan and Wharley Point

Start/Finish	Beach car park, Llansteffan (SN 354 108)
Distance	7km (4½ miles)
Ascent	150m (500ft)
Time	2hrs
Maps	Explorer 177
Refreshments	Cafés and pubs in Llansteffan
Public transport	Bus 227 Carmarthen–Llan-y-bri. Infrequent service, none Sun.

This most enjoyable walk could be split into two shorter circuits, if time is at a premium. Llansteffan has been a holiday resort for many years, with long expanses of sand edging the Tywi Estuary and stretching out past Wharley Point into Carmarthen Bay, attracting holidaymakers from the South Wales valleys. The walk itself is fairly gentle, with a lovely mix of coastal scenery, countryside and an attractive village.

Start from the stone surfaced car park, the first one encountered on approaching the estuary, and turn right along the surfaced footpath on top of the flood defence, heading towards **Llansteffan Castle**. This is a lovely way to start the walk, with attractive cottages to the right, a belt of sand dunes and the Tywi Estuary to the left and the ruins of the castle ahead. Just before reaching the children's playground, at the second surfaced car park, bear left and walk along the back of the beach for 100 metres, before turning right onto a surfaced lane that is followed for 20 metres to a flight of steps on the left.

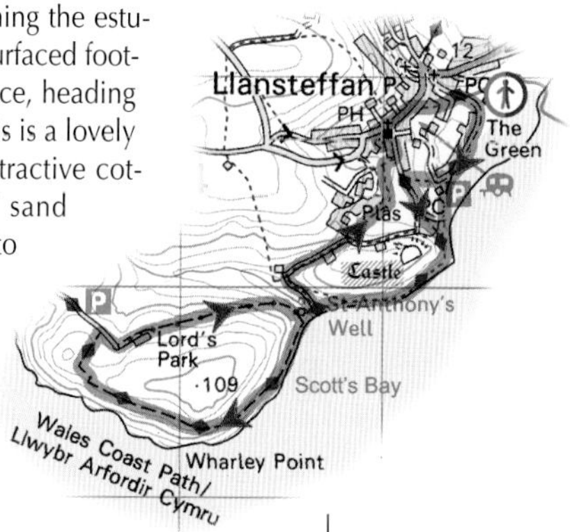

Diversion in the event of a high tide

During high spring tides, the beach walk may not be possible. In which case, bear right across the second car park to a waymarker post, climb steps and follow an enclosed footpath to a lane. Turn left along this, bearing left at a fork to rejoin the walk at the steps.

Climb the steps onto a footpath, bear left at a T-junction and proceed through woodland, with the ramparts of the castle up to the right and the estuary down to the left, to reach the lovely, secluded beach at **Scott's Bay**.

The impressive **house behind the beach**, named after Captain John Scott who lived in St Anthony's Cottage, enjoys one of the most beautiful locations in South Wales. It is rumoured that Richard Burton and Elizabeth Taylor have stayed here in the past.

Pass in front of the cottage and continue along the coastal footpath, soon passing **Wharley Point**, where a well-placed bench offers a chance of a rest while enjoying splendid vista.

The views from **Wharley Point** are truly breathtaking, out across Carmarthen Bay towards Gower, with Exmoor and even Lundy Island visible on a clear day. At low tide, the vast expanses of sand are exposed, but these are constantly shifting, silting up the river channels and forming sand bars across the estuary mouth, a headache for local shipping, which has declined rapidly over the years. However, the bay has been the scene of numerous shipwrecks in the past, with one such incident occurring in 1886 during severe southwesterly gales, when a four-masted iron barque, called the *Teviotdale* and loaded with South Wales coal bound for Bombay, foundered here with the loss of 17 of her crew. Due south from here, on the opposite side of the estuary, is Cefn Sidan Sands, from where the RAF operates an air weapons range. Hawke jet aircraft and Apache helicopters train here and it is a fairly common site to see Hercules transporters flying low over Llansteffan Castle, making approach and practice landings on the beach.

Eventually, the footpath swings rightwards, away from the coast, to reach a quiet lane which is followed to the right, past the National Trust's **Lord's Park Farm**. ▶ Keep left of all the farm buildings, soon joining an enclosed footpath with views of Llansteffan Castle directly ahead, pass through a field gate and walk along the top right edge of four fields. Pass through a gate at the end of the fourth field, walk along an enclosed footpath that descends towards Scott's Bay once more and a junction with the outward footpath.

A typical example of an 'estate' farm that came into being as common grazing land was enclosed and new gentry estates were organised into a system of home and tenant farms.

Enjoying the coastal footpath above Wharley Point

Turn left along the coastal footpath, past St Anthony's Cottage for a second time, but then turn immediately left along a track to the right of the cottage's garden and past **St Anthony's Well**, an ancient spring said to have healing properties. The track eventually swings right, in front of a house, then climbs steadily up the north side of Castle Hill, where it eventually becomes surfaced. Just beyond here, the now minor road swings rightwards, but go left off the track, over a stile and walk alongside the wall and fence surrounding **Plas Mansion**. ◀ At a fence corner, continue directly ahead, contouring round the field and heading towards houses in **Llansteffan** where two stiles in quick succession lead down onto Church Road. Turn left for 80 metres, then bear left into the grounds of **Llansteffan Church**.

To visit Llansteffan Castle, continue along the lane, bearing right up the access track to the castle and after visiting, retrace your steps back to the stile – see Walk 24 for more on the castle.

One train of thought is that the very attractive **Llansteffan Church** was established in the sixth century by St Ystyffan (an associate of the more eminent St Teilo), to whom it is now dedicated. Others believe the church to be of Norman origin, built in the 13th century and dedicated to St Stephen, a dedication that lasted for 800 years. The oldest part of the church is the nave, which does indeed date back to the 13th century and was probably erected at the same time as the castle was being enlarged. It is a Grade II listed building and despite various repairs taking place throughout the Victorian era, it did not receive a full restoration, resulting in much of its medieval character remaining intact, including traces of wall mural.

Walk across the churchyard, passing to the left of the church to enter High Street and turn right along this, passing the Sticks Hotel and Castle Inn, both on the left. Some 30 metres beyond the Village Store, go right at a public footpath sign, along an enclosed, surfaced footpath, turning left along a road then almost immediately right at the road junction. Where the road swings round to the right, go directly ahead back to the car park.

WALK 26

Laugharne North

Start/Finish	Castle car park, Laugharne (SN 301 106)
Distance	5km (3 miles)
Ascent	120m (390ft)
Time	1½hrs
Maps	Explorer 177
Refreshments	Cafés and pubs in Laugharne
Public transport	Bus 222 Pendine–Carmarthen. No service Sun.

This walk makes a lovely little outing. It explores the countryside immediately north of Laugharne by setting off beneath the ramparts of the castle, passing the Boathouse, home to Dylan Thomas for a time, then running close to the Afon Taf, through the grounds of the attractive Delacorse, before swinging back past the fine church of St Martins and back to Laugharne. The walk follows clear footpaths, tracks and lanes and would make a lovely pre-Sunday lunch ramble, or an outing when many footpaths are little more than streams. It can be linked with Walk 27.

Cross the pedestrian footbridge spanning the little River Coran and follow the well surfaced footpath beneath the impressive castle ramparts towards the **Afon Taf**, passing various seating areas with an array of carvings and art work. Where the footpath ends, climb up a natural stone staircase to reach a flight of stone steps that lead up to Cliff Road where Dylan Thomas's writing shed is situated.

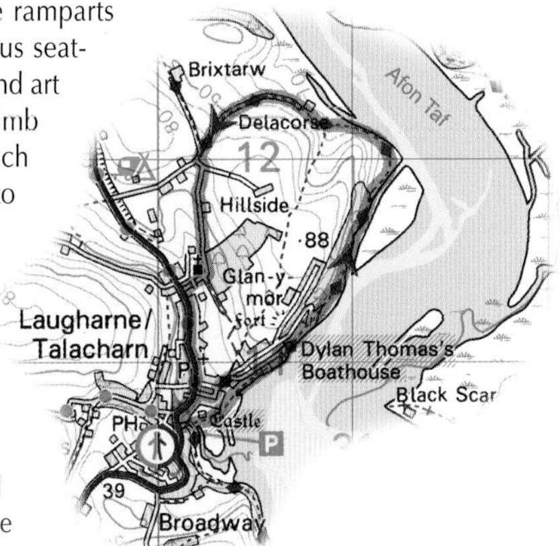

Dylan Thomas's **writing shed**, once the garage to the Boathouse, has a window that affords astounding views over the Taf Estuary and across Carmarthen Bay towards the

Gower, views that inspired the poet to write some of his finest lines, some of which can be read at points on this walk.

Diversion in the event of a high tide

If the tide is high, this initial section is impassable. At such times it is necessary to walk along Wogan Street, passing the entrance to the castle, then turn right into Market Lane, right again at the end into Victoria Street and right again into Cliff Road to rejoin the walk at the writing shed.

Bear right along Cliff Road, passing above the Boathouse, home to Dylan, his wife Caitlin and their three children from 1949 to 1953. Continue on along Dylan's Walk, which runs through woodland above the Taf, cross a road onto the continuation footpath that leads to a kissing gate giving access to a field. Head on along the right hand fence line, still with the river to the right, cross a wooden footbridge spanning a stream at the far end, pass through a gate and walk on towards buildings at **Delacorse** directly ahead. Keep left of the house and join its access drive, which climbs steadily for 640 metres to a junction with a surfaced lane and here turn left for a further 40 metres to reach another road junction. Go left

The Boathouse, home to writer Dylan Thomas

again, passing the entrance to Delacorse Uchaf and continuing for 500 metres, where an iron gate, at the end of a wall on the right, leads down steps into the grounds of **St Martin's Church**, a solid stone building with some fine stained glass windows.

> **St Martin's** is best known as being the final resting place of Dylan Thomas and his wife Caitlin, whose grave is marked by a simple white cross in the extension of the churchyard. It is found by crossing a footbridge over a lane on the south side of the church.

After visiting, re-cross the footbridge, turn left through the lychgate and walk along the cobbled lane down to the A4066. Turn left onto this road to walk along Laugharne's main street, passing Brown's Hotel, one of Thomas' favourite watering holes, now a rather smart hotel and restaurant, the attractive Town Hall, crowned with a fine clock tower, and onto the entrance to the **castle**.

> Standing sentinel over the Taf Estuary, **Laugharne Castle**, an ancient relic from medieval times, is a magnificent spectacle and one well worth exploring. Built originally from local Old Red Sandstone in the 13th century, with later additions of green stone in the 15th and 16th centuries, the castle has a very mellow, distinctive look which Dylan Thomas described as being 'Brown as owls' in his 'Poem in October'. Towards the end of the 16th century, the castle was transformed from a virtual ruin into a fine Tudor mansion by the Elizabethan courtier, Sir John Perrot. Sadly, the renaissance of its fortunes was short-lived, because in 1644 it was captured by Royalists during the Civil War, but quickly retaken by Parliamentarians following gunfire and siege.

Continue along the road back to the car park.

WALK 27

Laugharne South

Start/Finish	Castle car park, Laugharne (SN 301 106)
Distance	5.5km (3½ miles)
Ascent	145m (470ft)
Time	1½–2hrs
Maps	Explorer 177
Refreshments	Cafés and pubs in Laugharne
Public transport	Bus 222 Pendine–Carmarthen. No service Sun.

This most enjoyable ramble explores the beautiful coast and countryside to south of Laugharne, the inspiration for many of Dylan Thomas' works and the town's most famous resident who described it as 'this timeless, mild, beguiling island of a town...there is nowhere like it anywhere at all'. The walk offers breathtaking views across the Taf Estuary towards the Gower before circling beneath Sir John's Hill, skirting Laugharne Burrows and returning to Laugharne via quiet tracks, lanes and footpaths. This walk can be linked with Walk 26.

This section is liable to flooding at high tides. Check the notice board at the front of the car park for tide times and heights.

Facing the estuary from the car park bear right, past a small public garden with a carved bust of Dylan Thomas, and walk parallel to the little River Coran, along the surfaced track that heads towards woodland on Sir John's Hill. ◂ Just before the pumping station, go right at a footpath sign for 'Dylan's Birthday Walk'.

Originally known as **New Walk**, it created in 1856 by Laugharne Corporation, allowing the town's cocklers to access their shares of the valuable cockle beds on the upper and lower marshes when high tides prevented access along the shore.

Climb up through woodland cloaking **Sir John's Hill**, to eventually reach a fork in the path with an information board, bench and superb views over the mouth of the Afon Taf.

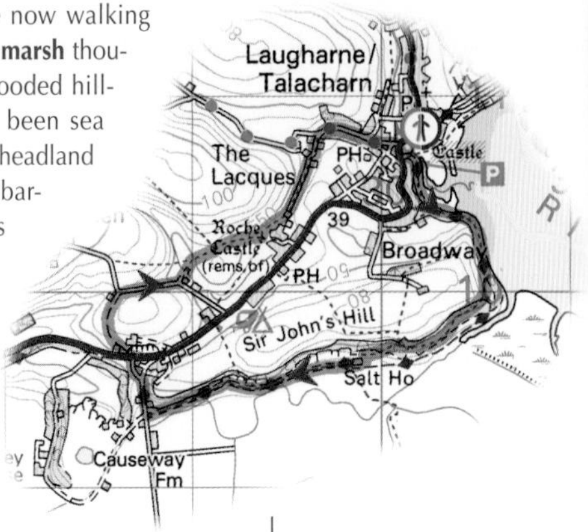

The land over which you are now walking would have been **flooded salt marsh** thousands of years ago and the wooded hillside to the right would have been sea cliffs. However, the limestone headland at Pendine acted as a natural barrier, allowing millions of tonnes of sand to build up under the prevailing southwesterly winds and waves, so creating one of the largest sand dune systems in South Wales. As the sand dunes built up, preventing the sea from inundating the area, the salt marsh began to dry out and a very important ecological community evolved.

From the viewpoint, go left on a steeply descending footpath that leads to steps and a pedestrian gate. Once through, the path levels out as it runs along the edge of salt marshes towards **Salt House Farm** but, on approaching the farm, veer left through a kissing gate and pass left of the farm buildings, soon joining its access drive which leads out to a minor road in front of the quarry at Coygan.

Until demolished by quarrying in the 20th century, **Coygan Cave** had been the home to creatures now extinct in the British Isles and indeed in the world in some cases. The cave was excavated a total of five times, the latter being in 1963, just before its own extinction. A range of animal bones were found, including cave bear, woolly rhinoceros, bison, Irish elk, reindeer and hyena, the latter probably being responsible for dragging most of the bones into the cave after scavenging from dead carcases. Stone tools were also found and dated to about 45,000 years old, indicating human occupation from the Neanderthal period.

Turn right to reach the A4066, crossing to the stony track on the opposite side which runs past the property known as Hill Crest and climbs steadily between fields to a junction with a quiet lane. Go right, descending steadily for approximately 400 metres to a track on the left, that passes alongside an isolated house, and climbs gently through a field, but where the track swings left, continue straight ahead on a less distinct grassy track, now descending steadily towards the left and houses visible in Broadway.

Towards the end of the field bear rightwards, passing an isolated electricity pole, to reach a hedge corner (waymarker) and here go left along the hedge-line, following a sunken footpath through woodland, eventually climbing a stile beside a gate, followed by a footbridge over a stream, passing to the left of a house before joining its access track that leads out to the minor road. Turn right along this and follow it back into Laugharne, with the castle soon coming into view and passing an old water pump on the way with the sign 'The Lacques' above.

Boats moored in the tidal River Coran, Laugharne

WALK 28

Pendine to Amroth

Start/Finish	Museum of Speed, Pendine (SN 235 080); New Inn, Amroth (SN 172 072)
Distance	8km (5 miles)
Ascent	465m (1520ft)
Time	3hrs
Maps	Explorer 177
Refreshments	Pubs and cafés in Pendine and Amroth
Public transport	Bus 222 Carmarthen–Pendine; bus 351 Tenby–Amroth–Pendine, limited service, non Sun.

This section of the Wales Coast Path is very different from any other part that falls within the confines of Carmarthenshire, being more reminiscent of large sections of the Pembrokeshire Coast Path, which it joins at Amroth. Despite its relatively short length, it is quite tough, with several steep climbs onto exposed cliffs and descents into quiet valleys. Once away from the tourist 'honey pot' of Pendine, this beautiful coastal walk soon takes on an air of quiet solitude with several points of interest along the way, including the Museum of Speed in Pendine, the remains of Iron Age hill forts, relics from the Second World War, superb wildlife and outstanding views for much of the way. If you are using both private and public transport to access the walk, it may be advisable to use the free parking at Amroth and catch the Number 351 bus service to the start in Pendine.

Museum of Speed in Pendine was opened in 1996 and focuses on the use of Pendine Sands for land speed attempts and racing. In the early 1900s the sands were used as a venue for car and motorcycle races and from 1922 the annual Welsh TT motorcycle event was held

map continues on page 159

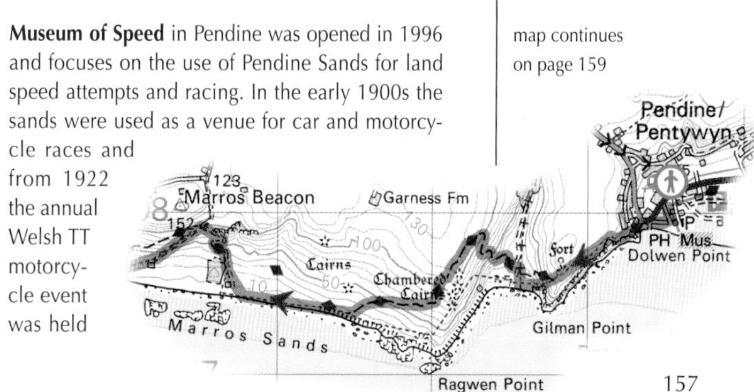

Pendine Sands from Dolwen Point

there. The firm flat surface of the beach created a racetrack that was both straighter and smoother than many major roads at the time, with *Motor Cycle* magazine describing it as 'The finest natural speedway imaginable'.

From the Museum of Speed, walk onto the footpath above the beach and bear right, passing pubs and cafés until you reach a steep flight of steps, at the very right hand end of the promenade, leading onto the limestone headland of **Dolwen Point**, furnished with a very well positioned bench.

After regaining your breath, the walk along the cliff top is fairly easy going, with a variety of wild plants thriving in the shade of the blackthorn bushes along the way. On the short ascent to **Gilman Point**, the path passes through the defensive banks and ditches of an Iron Age fort, before making the steady descent to Morfa Bychan. Cross the access track to the beach and walk past the now decaying concrete structures that are the remains of 'Exercise Jantzen'.

> During the **summer of 1943**, hundreds of troops in landing craft, with tanks and all necessary equipment, repeatedly practiced storming the beach here at Morfa Bychan. This secret Second World War exercise, code named 'Exercise Jantzen' and reputedly watched by Winston Churchill, was designed to prepare troops for the planned Normandy landings. The huge slab of concrete at the back of the beach, with its exposed and rusting iron work, along with a few pyramid-shaped 'dragon's teeth' tank buster blocks, is all that now remains.

Follow the grassy footpath that zigzags steadily up the opposite side of the valley, keeping left at the junction with a track near the top of the rise, to eventually reach a well waymarked kissing gate. Once through, the path begins to make an easy, serpentine descent through rough, gorse covered pasture, crosses a series of board walks over boggy ground, home to newts and toads, to reach a bifurcation. Keep right here, following the Wales Coast Path waymarkers, to eventually cross a stream and climb a stile beside a gate.

The path now climbs steadily through woodland, which are a mass of blue in spring when the bluebells flower, to reach a metal kissing gate leading onto the access drive to buildings at Marros Mill and here go right, climbing steeply towards **Marros Beacon**. Pass through another kissing gate, cross the access drive to the aptly named, but beautifully situated Underhill, to a pedestrian gate on the opposite side and follow a very pleasant, grassy footpath, with magnificent views over **Marros Sands**, the Gower, Worms Head, westward to

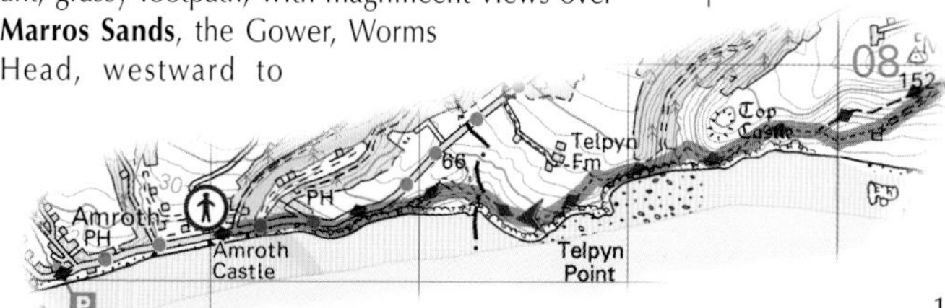

Saundersfoot and Tenby and on a clear day, even to Devon, Lundy Island and Cornwall.

> At the end of the last Ice Age, the **sea levels** along the coast began to rise, submerging the marshes and forests that once occupied the bay. At low tide, it is possible to see the remains of tree stumps from these ancient forests, samples of which, along with peat from beds found below high tide level, have been radiocarbon dated to around 3000BC.

Local legend has it that the last wild wolf in Wales was killed here in Teague's Wood.

Eventually, the pleasant undulations cease, to be replaced by another steep climb to **Top Castle** and the site of another Iron Age hill fort known as Napps Camp. A short section of lovely cliff top walking now follows before the steep, zigzag descent into Teague's Wood, where a footbridge spans the stream in the bottom. ◂

The climb out of valley feels quite tough, but is rewarded at the top by views westward to the walks final destination, Amroth. From the brow of the hill, where there are fine views westward past Telpyn cliffs into Pembrokeshire, a long, gentle descent ensues, across **Telpyn Point**, to a footbridge spanning a stream, with a short flight of steps opposite that climb to a track heading down to Telpyn Beach. Go left for 5 metres, then right up a final flight of steps, where a line of wind bent trees and bushes guides the direction of travel westward into a grassy meadow and walk round the left edge of this. The indistinct footpath eventually runs parallel with the road to reach a gate, at the far end of the pasture, and once through turn left along the road, passing a house called Merryfields, to descend to the New Inn in **Amroth** and fine views along the extensive golden sands of Amroth Beach.

WALK 29

Meidrim

Start/Finish	Car park in Meidrim on east side of the river bridge (SN 291 208)
Distance	9km (5½ miles)
Ascent	180m (590ft)
Time	3hrs
Maps	Explorer 177
Refreshments	Pub in Meidrim
Public transport	Bus 224 Carmarthen–Whitland and bus 225 Carmarthen–Tre-lech. Both services infrequent, none Sun.

Very enjoyable and fairly easy, this walk explores the attractive countryside to the north of Meidrim. It follows largely clear footpaths and tracks through farmland, along with short sections of quiet lanes and reaches the tiny hamlet of Gellywen in the tranquil tree lined valley of the Afon Cynin. Meidrim, from where the walk starts, is an attractive village, with an impressive Norman church that, like many in Carmarthenshire, lacks a tower. The village is situated just north of St Clears, on a crossroads of the B4298 and B4299.

The area around **Meidrim** has been settled since prehistoric times and the origins of the village probably lie in the Iron Age, over 2000 years ago. Since then, Christianity has had a big part to play in the shaping of Meidrim and evidence would suggest that this may stretch back to the Age of the Saints during the fifth to 11th centuries. The current church, dedicated to St David, stands on the site of an ancient fortification.

From the car park, turn left along the road, crossing the **Afon Dewi Fawr**, then go right immediately beyond the Fountain Inn and along the Newcastle Emlyn road. ▶

To visit the church, continue over the crossroads, walk uphill, along the Llanboidy road until you reach a flight of steps on the right leading to the church hall and churchyard.

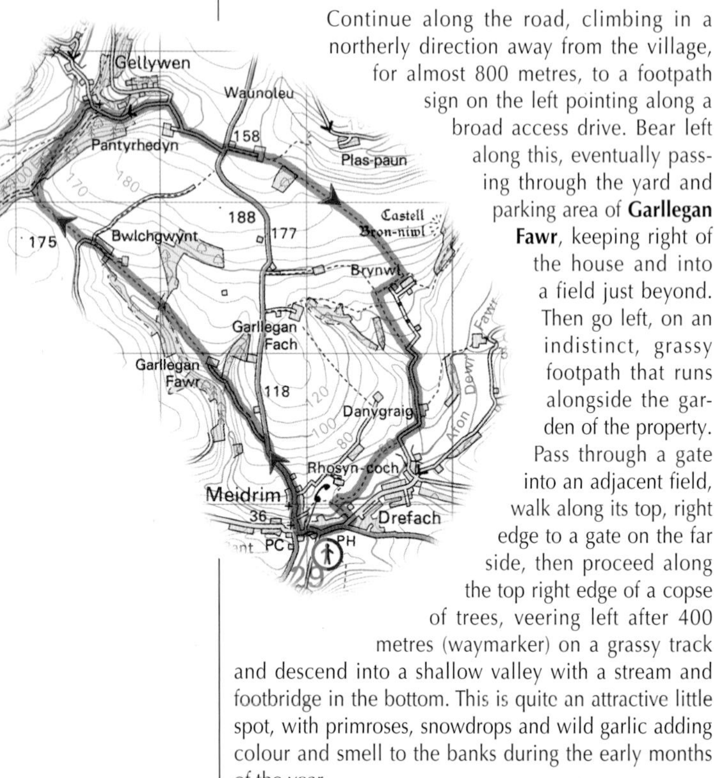

Continue along the road, climbing in a northerly direction away from the village, for almost 800 metres, to a footpath sign on the left pointing along a broad access drive. Bear left along this, eventually passing through the yard and parking area of **Garllegan Fawr**, keeping right of the house and into a field just beyond. Then go left, on an indistinct, grassy footpath that runs alongside the garden of the property. Pass through a gate into an adjacent field, walk along its top, right edge to a gate on the far side, then proceed along the top right edge of a copse of trees, veering left after 400 metres (waymarker) on a grassy track and descend into a shallow valley with a stream and footbridge in the bottom. This is quite an attractive little spot, with primroses, snowdrops and wild garlic adding colour and smell to the banks during the early months of the year.

Cross the bridge, proceeding along the footpath, which climbs to a kissing gate, then walk across a field, keeping just left of the path of the overhead power lines and heading for buildings at **Bwlchgwynt**. Pass through a waymarked gateway onto an enclosed track, pass through two more gateways, cross a track and go through a pedestrian gate, then veer slightly right through a sloping pasture to reach a pedestrian gate leading onto the farm access drive. Go left along the access drive, passing farm buildings and at a junction of tracks, 100 metres beyond the farm, continue directly ahead along a lane, but where it swings left, turn right through a gate leading into a long, narrow field. Walk along the right edge of this, passing through a gate at the far end that leads onto a rough track skirting the top edge of a wood before descending along a steep sided valley with fabulous views towards the hamlet of Gellywen and over the Cynin Valley. Descend past a small quarry on the right, cross a stony forestry track onto the continuation footpath and continue on down to join the road in **Gellywen**, opposite the chapel.

The hamlet of **Gellywen** is little more than a scattering of houses in the lovely, tranquil tree-lined valley of the Afon Cynin. The largest building of note is the Ainon Baptist Chapel, built in 1828 and rebuilt in 1880. The baptismal trough, situated to the right of the chapel, is quit unique in that the trough is fed directly by a stream that runs through the chapel grounds.

The bridge and Fountain Inn in Meidrim

Views from a gate on the approach to Bwlchgwynt

Turn right along the road, climbing quite steeply at first, out of the valley, to reach a T-junction with the B4299 and turn left for a few metres before going right along the surfaced access drive to **Waun-oleu-fâch**. Go through a gate, just beyond Waun oleu-fâch, onto a rough continuation track past outbuildings, to reach a second gate after 50 metres leading into a field and walk along its right edge. Proceed along the right edge of a second field and a third, but in this field, keep walking around its boundary to reach a gate, 30 metres left of its top right hand corner. Walk along the right side of a fourth field and pass through a gate at its far end onto an enclosed track that descends steadily into the valley of the Afon Dewi Fawr.

Over to the left from here is the site of **Castell Bron Niwl**, an Iron Age fort, built at a point where the slope down into the valley steepens, forming a natural defence. It is probably best described as a defended enclosure, some 85 metres in diameter, which incorporates a steep slope into its defensive circuit, rather than a promontory fort. The site was described as 'well preserved', prior to 1983, but sadly during that year the new landowner decided to bulldoze the ramparts into the ditch and plough over the site, virtually demolishing this 2500-year-old monument.

Follow the track round to the right, passing the very attractive buildings at **Brynwl** over to the left, but where the track swings round to the left, proceed directly ahead, over a stile and along the bottom edge of a field. Negotiate a pair of stiles on the far side, turn left through a pasture and through the right hand of a pair of gates at the bottom, proceeding in the same direction down the left side of the next pasture. Veer slightly left part way down, onto an enclosed track between fields, to reach twin pedestrian gates leading onto a lane and continue on along this. Pass buildings at **Danygraig**, cross a small stream, but part way round the next left hand bend, go right through a gate (waymarker), climb a stile and walk along the bottom edge of a low bank. After 200 metres climb a stile on the left and once over, turn right along the edge of a field, negotiating a stile and footbridge in the far corner, then follow the obvious footpath through a copse of trees, with the pretty Afon Dewi Fawr to the left. Climb a stile, turn left over a footbridge just beyond and walk across playing fields on **Meidrim** village green, turning right on the far side, along a rough track that climbs up to reach a road in the village. Turn right along the road back to the start.

WALK 30

Llanboidy

Start/Finish	Public car park, Llanboidy (SN 217 231)
Distance	10km (6 miles)
Ascent	210m (670ft)
Time	3–4hrs
Maps	Explorer 177
Refreshments	Pub in Llanboidy
Public transport	Bus 221 Carmarthen–Llanboidy–Login. Services Wed and Sat only.

Llanboidy is a fairly small village, lying in the valley of the Afon Gronw and surrounded by gently rolling hills in the western most fringes of Carmarthenshire. It is best known today for the organic cheese that bears its name and which is made just to the west of the village at Cilowen Uchaf. The walk is fairly gentle, with one long but steady climb out of the Afon Gronw Valley and an equally long but steady descent back to Llanboidy. Most of the walk follows clearly marked footpaths, tracks and quiet country lanes, with far reaching views in places towards the Preselli Hills in Pembrokeshire and the Carmarthen Fan in the Brecon Beacons.

From the car park, cross the road mto the pedestrian gate and footpath opposite and follow this along the left edge of a field. To the right is a mound that suggests the remains of a **motte-and-bailey castle**, but strangely, no historical evidence has ever come to light regarding the existence of a castle here. Two footbridges are soon crossed, one spanning a rather boggy area and the other a small tributary of the Afon Gronw, before continuing along the left edge of the next three fields. Walk in the same direction through the centre of a fourth field, passing an isolated 'standing stone' en route and heading to the right side of buildings at Parsonage. Descend a bank on the far side of the field, cross a footbridge over a stream, then bear right across a field to the opposite hedge line and walk rightwards beside this, eventually reaching steps and a stile leading onto the access drive to Parsonage.

Turn right along the drive to a T-junction with a lane, then go right again, descending to cross the **Afon Gronw** and passing buildings at Ddol before reaching another T-junction. Go right, with views towards Llanboidy across the fields to the right and at another T-junction, just south of Llanboidy, bear left away from the village on the road towards St Clears. After 400 metres, bear right by a footpath sign and along a broad track that descends to a **ford** and footbridge across the Afon Gronw. Once over, turn right along a rough track which climbs steadily out of the valley and where this swings sharp left into a field, go straight ahead to a stile and once over walk up the left edge of a large, sloping field. At the top of the field turn right along the hedge line to reach its top right hand corner, where a stile gives access to the next huge field. Walk up the right side of this, with distant views to the east across the rolling hills of Carmarthenshire towards the Carmarthen Fan and western fringes of the Brecon Beacons.

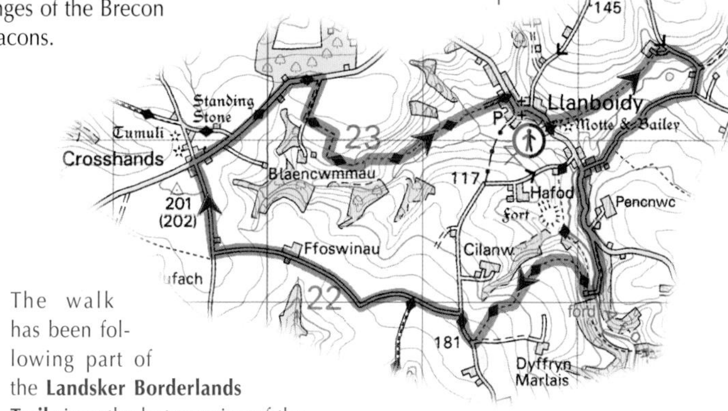

The walk has been following part of the **Landsker Borderlands Trail** since the last crossing of the Afon Gronw, in the bottom of the valley. The trail is a long distance trail that roughly follows the Landsker Line, a 'non-visible' border that divided the Welsh speaking people to the north from the English speaking people to the south during the

Norman invasions of southwest Wales. The line changed position many times over the centuries, depending on the volatility of the 'neighbours', but it roughly stretched from St Bride's Bay in the west of Pembrokeshire, then followed a serpentine course eastwards across Carmarthenshire to reach the River Taf, just north of Laugharne on the fringes of Carmarthen Bay. During the complex period of conflict in the 11th and 12th centuries, more than 50 castles or fortifications were constructed along the line, both by invaders and defenders.

At the top of the field climb a stile onto a lane and bear right for 200 metres, then go left along another lane, now with views of the Preseli Hills in the north of Pembrokeshire. This quiet lane undulates steadily along a breezy hill, eventually reaching a T-junction in a little over 1.5km and here turn right to reach a crossroads at **Crosshands**.

Turn right at the crossroads, following the road for 1km then go right, opposite the entrance to Maesgwynne Holiday Cottages, and along a farm access drive.

The **holiday cottages** are built on the site of the former 18th-century Maesgwynne Mansion Estate, owned by Walter Rice Howell Powell MP who was Lord Lieutenant of Carmarthenshire and responsible for bringing the mains water supply to Llanboidy.

Shortly after the drive begins to descend, turn left by a footpath sign, passing through a gateway and climbing a stile into a field, then walk along the top, left edge of this and the next field to reach a stile beside a gate. Once over bear right down the side of another field, then go left along its lower boundary, with a narrow belt of trees to the right, and after 170 metres turn right and climb a stile beside a gate. Veer left along a broad, grassy footpath that leads pleasantly down to another stile giving access to sheep pens and, once through these, head down to the bottom right hand corner of the field with

Llanboidy Church

good views over **Llanboidy** directly ahead. Join a rough field track towards the end of the field, enclosed by trees, and follow this back towards the village, turning right at a junction with the road and passing the church on the left, dedicated to St Brynach, a sixth-century saint who founded a monastery at Nevern in Pembrokeshire. The church is medieval in origin, however, the chancel and north chapel are 19th-century restorations. Continue along the road back to the car park.

APPENDIX A

Walk summary table

Walk	Start/Finish	Distance	Ascent	Time	Maps	Page
1	Bronwydd	11km (7 miles)	260m (855ft)	3–4hrs	Explorer 177 and 185	24
2	Cenarth Falls	11km (7 miles)	305m (1005ft)	3–4hrs	Explorer 198	29
3	Drefach Felindre	10km (6 miles)	300m (980ft)	3–4hrs	Explorer 185	34
4	Llandysul	11km (7 miles)	195m (645ft)	3–4hrs	Explorer 185	39
5	Brechfa Forest West	14km (9 miles)	340m (1110ft)	4–5hrs	Explorer 186	46
6	National Botanic Garden of Wales	11km (7 miles)	295m (965ft)	3–4hrs	Explorer 186	51
7	Dryslwyn	14km (9 miles)	210m (695ft)	4–5hrs	Explorer 186	56
8	Llandeilo	8km (5 miles)	175m (575ft)	2½–3hrs	Explorer 186	61
9	Dolaucothi	11km (7 miles)	410m (1345ft)	3–4hrs	Explorer 186 and 187	68
10	Cil-y-cwm	13km (8 miles)	390m (1280ft)	4–5hrs	Explorer 187	73
11	Crychan Forest	10.5km (6½ miles)	360m (1180ft)	3–4hrs	Explorer 187	78
12	Llandovery	5.5km (3½ miles)	55m (185ft)	2hrs	Explorer 187	84
13	Myddfai	11km (7 miles)	385m (1265ft)	3–4hrs	Outdoor Leisure 12	90
14	Usk Reservoir	8km (5 miles)	125m (405ft)	2–3hrs	Outdoor Leisure 12	95
15	Near Carn Goch	15km (9½ miles); or 9.5km (6 miles)	350m (1150ft); or 275m (900ft)	4–6hrs; or 3–4hrs	Outdoor Leisure 12	99

Walk	Start/Finish	Distance	Ascent	Time	Maps	Page
16	Carreg Cennen Castle	6.5km (4 miles)	230m (765ft)	2–2½hrs	Explorer 165 and 186	105
17	Near Llanddeusant	8½ miles (14km); or 11km (7 miles); or 15.5km (9½ miles)	685m (2245ft); or 545m (1780ft); or 700m (2315ft)	4–6hrs; or 3½–5½hrs; or 4½–6½hrs	Outdoor Leisure 12	110
18	Herbert's Quarry	14km (8½ miles)	515m (1690ft)	4–6hrs	Outdoor Leisure 12	114
19	Loughor Bridge/Llanelli North Dock	10.5km (6½ miles)	40m (125ft)	3–4hrs	Explorer 164	120
20	Llanelli North Dock/ Burry Port Harbour	7km (4½ miles)	40m (125ft)	2–2½hrs	Explorer 164	124
21	Cwm Lliedi Reservoir and Parc Howard	9km (5½ miles)	210m (690ft)	3hrs	Explorer 178	127
22	Burry Port Harbour/ Kidwelly	17km (10½ miles)	70m (230ft)	4–6hrs	Explorer 164	133
23	Kidwelly	13km (8 miles)	295m (970ft)	4–5hrs	Explorer 177	137
24	Llansteffan	4km (2½ miles)	150m (490ft)	1½hrs	Explorer 177	144
25	Llansteffan	7km (4½ miles)	150m (500ft)	2hrs	Explorer 177	147
26	Laugharne	5km (3 miles)	120m (390ft)	1½hrs	Explorer 177	151
27	Laugharne	5.5km (3½ miles)	145m (470ft)	1½–2hrs	Explorer 177	154
28	Pendine/Amroth	8km (5 miles)	465m (1520ft)	3hrs	Explorer 177	157
29	Meidrim	9km (5½ miles)	180m (590ft)	3hrs	Explorer 177	161
30	Llanboidy	10km (6 miles)	210m (670ft)	3–4hrs	Explorer 177	166

APPENDIX B

Useful contacts

General

One of the most useful websites for finding information on accommodation, places to stay, transport and a number of other categories is the Carmarthenshire County Council website, www.carmarthenshire.gov.uk. In the 'Your Council' section you will find bus and train information, along with downloadable timetables, maps of all bus routes and train services within the county. In the 'Discover' section there are lists of accommodation providers, events, things to do and so on. There are also the same options in the Welsh language.

Public transport

Carmarthenshire County Council Transport Unit provides comprehensive information on all bus and train services within the county. Use www.carmarthenshire.gov.uk or call tel 01267 234567. They can also be reached at Passenger Transport Unit, Parc Myrddin, Carmarthen, SA31 1HQ.

Information on train services can also be found at www.arrivatrainswales.co.uk or by calling tel 08457 484940 (or tel 08456 040500 for information in the Welsh language).

Accommodation

Visit Wales (www.visit-wales.co.uk) has details of a wide range of possibilities and in all price ranges. You can also call tel 08708 300 306. As mentioned previously, the County Council website is also a good source of information and ranges from 5-star hotels to camping and bunkhouses. www.discovercarmarthenshire.com will take you directly to the County Council website where there is a link to the accommodation listings. Another website of interest is www.wheretoincarmarthenshire.co.uk (or call tel 01554 821 350) which also has many possibilities in all price ranges.

Tourist information centres

There are three main tourist information centres spread throughout the county, all of which can offer detailed advice on places to stay, public transport, maps and leaflets for the local area. All are served by the same County Council website given above.

Carmarthen

Adjacent to County Hall
Carmarthen
SA31 1JP
Tel 01267 231557

Llandovery

Heritage Centre
KingsRd
Llandovery
SA20 0AW
Tel 01550 720693

Millennium Coast Park Llanelli

Discovery Centre
North Dock
Llanelli
SA15 2LK
Tel 01554 777744

LISTING OF CICERONE GUIDES

BRITISH ISLES CHALLENGES, COLLECTIONS AND ACTIVITIES

The Book of the Bivvy
The Book of the Bothy
The End to End Trail
The Mountains of England and Wales: 1&2
The National Trails
The Relative Hills of Britain
The Ridges of England, Wales and Ireland
The UK Trailwalker's Handbook
The UK's County Tops
Three Peaks, Ten Tors

UK CYCLING

20 Classic Sportive Rides
South West England
South East England
Border Country Cycle Routes
Cycling in the Cotswolds
Cycling in the Hebrides
Cycling in the Peak District
Cycling in the Yorkshire Dales
Cycling the Pennine Bridleway
Mountain Biking in the Lake District
Mountain Biking in the Yorkshire Dales
Mountain Biking on the North Downs
Mountain Biking on the South Downs
The C2C Cycle Route
The End to End Cycle Route
The Lancashire Cycleway

SCOTLAND

Backpacker's Britain
Central and Southern Scottish Highlands
Northern Scotland
Ben Nevis and Glen Coe
Great Mountain Days in Scotland
Not the West Highland Way
Scotland's Best Small Mountains
Scotland's Far West
Scotland's Mountain Ridges
Scrambles in Lochaber
The Ayrshire and Arran Coastal Paths
The Border Country
The Cape Wrath Trail
The Great Glen Way
The Hebrides
The Isle of Mull
The Isle of Skye
The Pentland Hills
The Skye Trail
The Southern Upland Way
The Speyside Way
The West Highland Way
Walking Highland Perthshire
Walking in Scotland's Far North
Walking in the Angus Glens
Walking in the Cairngorms
Walking in the Ochils, Campsie Fells and Lomond Hills
Walking in the Southern Uplands
Walking in Torridon
Walking Loch Lomond and the Trossachs
Walking on Harris and Lewis
Walking on Jura, Islay and Colonsay
Walking on Rum and the Small Isles
Walking on the Isle of Arran
Walking on the Orkney and Shetland Isles
Walking on Uist and Barra
Walking the Corbetts
1 South of the Great Glen
2 North of the Great Glen
Walking the Galloway Hills
Walking the Lowther Hills
Walking the Munros
1 Southern, Central and Western Highlands
2 Northern Highlands and the Cairngorms
Winter Climbs Ben Nevis and Glen Coe
Winter Climbs in the Cairngorms
World Mountain Ranges: Scotland

NORTHERN ENGLAND TRAILS

A Northern Coast to Coast Walk
Hadrian's Wall Path
The Dales Way
The Pennine Way

NORTH EAST ENGLAND, YORKSHIRE DALES AND PENNINES

Great Mountain Days in the Pennines
Historic Walks in North Yorkshire
South Pennine Walks
St Oswald's Way and St Cuthbert's Way
The Cleveland Way and the Yorkshire Wolds Way
The North York Moors
The Reivers Way
The Teesdale Way
The Yorkshire Dales
North and East
South and West
Walking in County Durham
Walking in Northumberland
Walking in the North Pennines
Walks in Dales Country
Walks in the Yorkshire Dales
Walks on the North York Moors – Books 1 & 2

NORTH WEST ENGLAND AND THE ISLE OF MAN

Historic Walks in Cheshire
Isle of Man Coastal Path
The Isle of Man
The Lune Valley and Howgills
The Ribble Way
Walking in Cumbria's Eden Valley
Walking in Lancashire
Walking in the Forest of Bowland and Pendle
Walking on the Isle of Man
Walking on the West Pennine Moors
Walks in Lancashire Witch Country
Walks in Ribble Country
Walks in Silverdale and Arnside
Walks in the Forest of Bowland

LAKE DISTRICT

Coniston Copper Mines
Great Mountain Days in the Lake District
Lake District: High Level and Fell Walks
Lake District: Low Level and Lake Walks
Lake District Winter Climbs
Lakeland Fellranger
The Central Fells
The Far-Eastern Fells
The Mid-Western Fells
The Near Eastern Fells
The Northern Fells
The North-Western Fells

The Southern Fells
The Western Fells
Roads and Tracks of the Lake District
Rocky Rambler's Wild Walks
Scrambles in the Lake District North & South
Short Walks in Lakeland
1 South Lakeland
2 North Lakeland
3 West Lakeland
The Cumbria Coastal Way
The Cumbria Way
Tour of the Lake District

DERBYSHIRE, PEAK DISTRICT AND MIDLANDS

High Peak Walks
Scrambles in the Dark Peak
The Star Family Walks
Walking in Derbyshire
White Peak Walks
The Northern Dales
The Southern Dales

SOUTHERN ENGLAND

Suffolk Coast & Heaths Walks
The Cotswold Way
The Great Stones Way
The Lea Valley Walk
The North Downs Way
The Peddars Way and Norfolk Coast Path
The Ridgeway National Trail
The South Downs Way
The South West Coast Path
The Thames Path
The Two Moors Way
Walking in Cornwall
Walking in Essex
Walking in Kent
Walking in Norfolk
Walking in Sussex
Walking in the Chilterns
Walking in the Cotswolds
Walking in the Isles of Scilly
Walking in the New Forest
Walking in the Thames Valley
Walking on Dartmoor
Walking on Guernsey
Walking on Jersey
Walking on the Isle of Wight
Walking on the North Wessex Downs
Walks in the South Downs National Park

WALES AND WELSH BORDERS

Glyndwr's Way
Great Mountain Days in Snowdonia
Hillwalking in Snowdonia
Hillwalking in Wales: 1&2
Offa's Dyke Path
Ridges of Snowdonia
Scrambles in Snowdonia
The Ascent of Snowdon
The Ceredigion and Snowdonia Coast Paths
Lleyn Peninsula Coastal Path
Pembrokeshire Coastal Path
The Severn Way
The Shropshire Hills
The Wales Coast Path
The Wye Valley Walk
Walking in Pembrokeshire
Walking in the Forest of Dean
Walking in the South Wales Valleys
Walking in the Wye Valley
Walking on Gower
Walking on the Brecon Beacons
Welsh Winter Climbs

INTERNATIONAL CHALLENGES, COLLECTIONS AND ACTIVITIES

Canyoning
Canyoning in the Alps
Europe's High Points
The Via Francigena: 1&2

EUROPEAN CYCLING

Cycle Touring in France
Cycle Touring in Ireland
Cycle Touring in Spain
Cycle Touring in Switzerland
Cycling in the French Alps
Cycling the Canal du Midi
Cycling the River Loire
The Danube Cycleway Vol 1
The Grand Traverse of the Massif Central
The Moselle Cycle Route
The Rhine Cycle Route
The Way of St James

AFRICA

Climbing in the Moroccan Anti-Atlas
Kilimanjaro
Mountaineering in the Moroccan High Atlas
The High Atlas
Trekking in the Atlas Mountains
Walking in the Drakensberg

ALPS – CROSS-BORDER ROUTES

100 Hut Walks in the Alps
Across the Eastern Alps: E5
Alpine Points of View
Alpine Ski Mountaineering
1 Western Alps
2 Central and Eastern Alps
Chamonix to Zermatt
Snowshoeing
Tour of Mont Blanc
Tour of the Matterhorn
Trekking in the Alps
Trekking in the Silvretta and Rätikon Alps
Walking in the Alps
Walks and Treks in the Maritime Alps

PYRENEES AND FRANCE/SPAIN CROSS-BORDER ROUTES

The GR10 Trail
The GR11 Trail – La Senda
The Mountains of Andorra
The Pyrenean Haute Route
The Pyrenees
The Way of St James: France & Spain
Walks and Climbs in the Pyrenees

AUSTRIA

The Adlerweg
Trekking in Austria's Hohe Tauern
Trekking in the Stubai Alps
Trekking in the Zillertal Alps
Walking in Austria

BELGIUM AND LUXEMBOURG

Walking in the Ardennes

EASTERN EUROPE

The High Tatras
The Mountains of Romania
Walking in Bulgaria's National Parks
Walking in Hungary

FRANCE

Chamonix Mountain Adventures
Ecrins National Park
Mont Blanc Walks
Mountain Adventures in the Maurienne
The Cathar Way
The GR20 Corsica
The GR5 Trail
The Robert Louis Stevenson Trail

Tour of the Oisans: The GR54
Tour of the Queyras
Tour of the Vanoise
Trekking in the Vosges and Jura
Vanoise Ski Touring
Via Ferratas of the French Alps
Walking in Corsica
Walking in Provence – East
Walking in Provence – West
Walking in the Auvergne
Walking in the Cevennes
Walking in the Dordogne
Walking in the Haute Savoie – North & South
Walking in the Languedoc
Walking in the Tarentaise and Beaufortain Alps
Walks in the Cathar Region

GERMANY

Germany's Romantic Road
Hiking and Biking in the Black Forest
Walking in the Bavarian Alps

HIMALAYA

Annapurna
Bhutan
Everest
Garhwal and Kumaon
Langtang with Gosainkund and Helambu
Manaslu
The Mount Kailash Trek
Trekking in Ladakh
Trekking in the Himalaya

ICELAND & GREENLAND

Trekking in Greenland
Walking and Trekking in Iceland

IRELAND

Irish Coastal Walks
The Irish Coast to Coast Walk
The Mountains of Ireland

ITALY

Gran Paradiso
Sibillini National Park
Shorter Walks in the Dolomites
Through the Italian Alps
Trekking in the Apennines
Trekking in the Dolomites
Via Ferratas of the Italian Dolomites: Vols 1 & 2
Walking in Abruzzo
Walking in Italy's Stelvio National Park
Walking in Sardinia
Walking in Sicily
Walking in the Central Italian Alps
Walking in the Dolomites
Walking in Tuscany
Walking in Umbria
Walking on the Amalfi Coast
Walking the Italian Lakes

MEDITERRANEAN

Jordan – Walks, Treks, Caves, Climbs and Canyons
The Ala Dag
The High Mountains of Crete
The Mountains of Greece
Treks and Climbs in Wadi Rum
Walking in Malta
Western Crete

NORTH AMERICA

British Columbia
The Grand Canyon
The John Muir Trail
The Pacific Crest Trail

SOUTH AMERICA

Aconcagua and the Southern Andes
Hiking and Biking Peru's Inca Trails
Torres del Paine

SCANDINAVIA

Walking in Norway

SLOVENIA, CROATIA AND MONTENEGRO

The Islands of Croatia
The Julian Alps of Slovenia
The Mountains of Montenegro
Trekking in Slovenia
Walking in Croatia
Walking in Slovenia: The Karavanke

SPAIN AND PORTUGAL

Mountain Walking in Southern Catalunya
The Mountains of Nerja
The Northern Caminos
Trekking through Mallorca
Walking in Madeira
Walking in Mallorca
Walking in Menorca
Walking in the Algarve
Walking in the Cordillera Cantabrica
Walking in the Sierra Nevada
Walking on Gran Canaria
Walking on La Gomera and El Hierro
Walking on La Palma
Walking on Lanzarote and Fuerteventura
Walking on Tenerife
Walking the GR7 in Andalucia
Walks and Climbs in the Picos de Europa

SWITZERLAND

Alpine Pass Route
Central Switzerland
The Bernese Alps
The Swiss Alps
Tour of the Jungfrau Region
Walking in the Bernese Oberland
Walking in the Valais
Walking in Ticino
Walks in the Engadine

TECHNIQUES

Geocaching in the UK
Indoor Climbing
Lightweight Camping
Map and Compass
Mountain Weather
Outdoor Photography
Polar Exploration
Rock Climbing
Sport Climbing
The Hillwalker's Guide to Mountaineering
The Hillwalker's Manual

MINI GUIDES

Alpine Flowers
Avalanche!
Navigating with a GPS
Navigation
Pocket First Aid and Wilderness Medicine
Snow

MOUNTAIN LITERATURE

8000 metres
A Walk in the Clouds
Unjustifiable Risk?

For full information on all our guides, books and eBooks, visit our website: **www.cicerone.co.uk**.